# FALSE ACCOUNTS - EXPOSING THE POST OFFICE COVER-UP

LANCE STEEN ANTHONY NIELSEN

'False Accounts - Exposing the Post Office Cover-Up'

Copyright © 2023 by Lance Steen Anthony Nielsen

All rights reserved.

No part of this book may be reproduced in any form or by any electronic or mechanical means, including information storage and retrieval systems, without written permission from the author, except for the use of brief quotations in a book review.

False Accounts was first performed at The Old Joint Stock, Birmingham in October 2022 and The Questors Theatre, Ealing, London in November 2022.

Although this play is based on a true story it should be read in the context of a work of satirical fiction and depiction of any named person should be viewed in this context of fact.

Cover and Jacket design by Dianne Bruckhardt

Photographs by Lance Nielsen and Alex Tabrizi

❋ Created with Vellum

*This play is dedicated to all the victims of the Post Office Scandal, too many to name here, whose lives were destroyed by this utter travesty.*

*I hope it brings you some small shred of comfort to know that we heard you.*

*With additional thanks to all those of you who came to support our production, knowing it would re-open old wounds...*

*This play is a voice for you all.*

―――――

*And for actor Lance Reddick - an outstanding talent, taken far too soon.*

# CONTENTS

| | |
|---|---|
| *Forewords* | vii |
| *Overview of The Horizon Post Office Scandal* | xi |
| *Composing the Score for False Accounts* | xv |
| *Taking on the story of the Horizon Post Office Scandal* | xix |
| *Cast & Crew of the 2022 & 2023 Productions of False Accounts* | xxix |
| | |
| Breaking down the Roles | 1 |
| 1. ACT I - FALSE ACCOUNTS | 3 |
| 2. ACT II - FALSE ACCOUNTS | 47 |
| | |
| *Acknowledgments* | 87 |
| *About the Author* | 89 |
| *Also by Lance Steen Anthony Nielsen* | 93 |

# FOREWORDS
## BY EDWARD KEVIN BROWN & DICKON TOLSON

**Edward Kevin Brown**

Firstly, I would just like to thank Lance for inviting me to say a few words on *False Accounts - Exposing The Post Office Cover-Up*. It's both an honour and a privilege to do so.

When we first heard about the production we were quite apprehensive about how this show would be portrayed. But after reading rave reviews from other former Sub-Postmasters (SPMs), my wife (and former SPM) Sharon and I were agreed in thinking that this would be a must see show. We made our minds up to see it at the Questors Theatre in Ealing.

We were definitely not disappointed!

Although the show was performed by professional actors we were surprised to learn later than they were on profit share, essentially meaning they had given up hours of their free time to stage this production. It is hard to articulate how much that meant to us.

The performers were absolutely superb, blending some really hard hitting aspects of our journey with light hearted banter, which had the audience in fits of laughter one minute and heartfelt tears of emotion the next.

We made a point of speaking to as many of the audience as possible and those who attended were in awe of this amazing, hard hitting production. We were all in agreement that it was sheer brilliance. An outstanding, 5 star production from start to finish.

When the curtain came down, it was a massive relief that such a show could be so precise in portraying all aspects of the plight that we suffered. All consequences as a result of the horrendous actions of Post Office Limited – The Nation's most trusted brand.

Well we all know what that means - Win at all costs!

Hopefully I'm speaking on behalf of all those involved who attended these performances, when I say that it was a brilliantly crafted show. You really need to see it to appreciate all of the fabulous work put in by the writer and the entire cast.

It truly was an absolutely fantastic tribute to all of the wronged former Subpostmasters.

We are still waiting for our justice to be served. Unfortunately, I am afraid to say that it will be a very long process. It's already been too long for some of us to see it reach its final conclusion and more will undoubtedly pass away before they're fully vindicated and compensated.

Finally I would like to say a massive thank you to all of the Production Team who contributed to the show. It enables everyone to see at first hand, the travesty of the brutal attack by the post office on the INNOCENT.

*Kevin and Sharon Brown, former Subpostmasters of our nations most trusted brand.*

## Dickon Tolson

Theatre should entertain, but it should also educate and sometimes even wrestle with the authority of the day. False Accounts does all of these things.

Lance has often written about issues of social justice, or more accurately injustice, but this is his first satire. I have always loved political satire, from Spitting Image to Have I Got News For You. Political satire can make a mockery of things that have very heavy gravitas, but it is often funny because it's true, and hitting that raw nerve is what emphasises the true points underlying such satire.

The Post Office Horizon scandal is one of the most widespread and enduring scandals of our times. It has been ignored and perpetuated by successive heads of state and leaders of what was 'our Royal Mail'. It seems representative of the erosion of many of our services and institutions as the world seeks to privatise and monetise everything, and as the Post Office became a corporate entity beholden to corporate expectations, the morals and principles that distinguished it previously were discarded.

People feel undervalued and powerless in the face of companies that cower to their shareholders to provide dividends and so ignore, and in this case oppress, their employees and customers. It is representative of the separation between the rich and the poor, the haves and the have-nots.

We are but cows and bees to provide their milk and honey.

And so, when Lance brought this play to the other half of the Outcasts creative (me) we felt that this was a 'must do' play. It has been a tough road, as this small band of players brought this script to life for the stage. Unfunded and unsupported, we have managed thus far to put on two runs of this play, in Birmingham and Ealing, which was in itself a triumph.

One of the doubts of tackling this issue as a satire was that this is a very serious issue, and we didn't want to make light of it, but the humour actually brings the issue home more deftly. The reservations we had though were soon quashed and washed away when the people most affected by this torrid episode came to see the play. The Subpostmasters had suffered for years, unheard, unbelieved, frustrated and ignored.

Some doubted themselves whether they wanted to go through the process of seeing it, but as we came out from the dressing room night after night to open arms and tears of sadness and joy, we knew this was needed as much for them as it was to raise the issue. We were left with the feeling that we had to embark upon this journey again, and so we look forward to a third run in Barnes, God and the universe willing.

**Dickon Tolson - Co-Founder of The Outcasts Creative**

# OVERVIEW OF THE HORIZON POST OFFICE SCANDAL

To fully understand the complexity, scale and many facets of the problems that allowed this terrible travesty of injustice to take place, you have to go back to the very beginning. In 1999 Post Office Limited sub-contracted IT Service Management Company Fujitsu to design and install a computerised system in every Post Office branch across the country. Fujitsu were awarded the contract because their bid was the cheapest, but their track record did not suggest they were best suited to install such a system. The most experienced company, IBM, had their bid rejected.

Designed to run the books of every branch and revolutionise the Post Office network, this new system was prone to bugs and errors from very beginning. It was a system which could cause phantom transactions and inaccurate accounting, a system which could leave the owner of a Post Office branch liable for substantial sums of 'missing' money. It was a system that the hierarchy of Fujitsu continued to convey was working properly. It was a system which the management hierarchy of Post Office Limited constantly placed blind faith in, despite growing evidence that all was not well within its design.

That system was called Horizon, and the issues with the system rapidly grew from impacting just a few dozen Post Office owners to several hundred all over the United Kingdom. Presently that number has increased exponentially and more cases are coming to light all the time.

So where had this missing money all gone? The thing you need to understand is that this money wasn't missing, it had in fact never been stolen in the first place but the Subpostmasters contract made them legally liable for any shortfall on their books. The sums they owed due to these faults in most cases were not small amounts either. Many of the victims would find their weekly balance down by thousands, often tens of thousands of pounds. Worse still, Post Office Limited (POL for short) had an entire department set up to prosecute such individuals. Their role was not to seek out the truth in each case but solely to get back any money owed, secure criminal convictions of the former Subpostmasters and protect the Horizon brand at any cost. As far as they were concerned Horizon was a completely robust system and the Subpostmasters who complained about their mysterious shortfalls were criminals.

Subpostmasters were arrested, made bankrupt, lost their homes, had marriages and lives destroyed, and some committed suicide. Their complaints and protests fell on deaf ears and were met with total indifference by the very systems and people that were put in place to protect them. Even in recent years when it became blatantly obvious to those at the top of POL that the Horizon system was not as 'completely robust' as they had been led to believe, rather than confront and address the problem head on, they took steps to cover it up. A state of almost wilful blindness towards the issue existed among the senior management which still continues among many of their staff to this day.

Huge sums of money were recovered from bankrupted former Subpostmasters. Properties, cars and savings were confiscated to line the coffers of Post Office Limited. All while their upper management were paid hefty salaries. In addition to compensation, all of this money and chattels should be returned.

Furthermore it has since come to light that there was an uneasy tone of racial prejudice at work within different levels of the same system. One witness to the Post Office Inquiry who was a former employee of the Horizon Helpline described a workplace culture where Subpostmasters who called in with accents of a certain ethnicity were described collectively as 'Patels' by members of staff, including some of the management. 'I've another Patel on the line...' he said they would often say to one another.

In the courts, those Subpostmasters of a non-white ethnicity who received criminal convictions were often given a more lengthy prison sentence or larger fines than their caucasian counterparts. While this didn't happen consistently across the board, if you examine the data, it is an uncomfortable trend that is certainly visible on paper.

Ultimately 555 former Subpostmasters would successfully sue Post Office Limited and win their case in the High Court, but the damage done to many was permanent. Several victims of what would become known as *The Horizon Post Office Scandal* did not live to see their criminal convictions quashed and their reputations restored. Many others have since died while awaiting their compensation in what some have described as the most convoluted scheme possible.

There's a huge number of villains and heroes in this story, too many to all get mentioned/portrayed in our play. Top of the list where the latter are concerned have to be the former Subpostmasters themselves. The resilience, courage and determination they have shown is nothing short of amazing. Many banded together and formed the Justice For Postmasters Alliance (JFSA) under the leadership of Alan Bates, a former Subpostmaster who had challenged POL and their actions from day one. This group would eventually form *'the 555'* a group of former Subpostmasters who would take POL to court. Others, completely unaware of those facing a similar dilemma fought battles of their own against a giant corporate entity.

Outside of the former Post Office owners, Journalists Nick Wallace and Rebecca Thompson from Computer Weekly were among the first to start reporting on this story while the rest of the media completely ignored it. The pair continue to collaborate on a Podcast that covers the Public Inquiry and the scandal in some considerable detail. Wallace has written an excellent book on the subject - *'The Great Post Office Scandal'* which we highly recommend you read.

There are also the lawyers and university lecturers who specialise in law. They have been breaking down all the illegal activity that Post Office Limited and those who work for them have been conducting over the years of the scandal. The list of potential offences is very long in this regard. Forensic Accounting experts Ian Henderson and Ron Warmington could have easily toed the Post Office line when they submitted their report. They did not and have become among the greatest allies of the former Subpostmasters. Lord Arbuthnot was the first MP to get directly involved - his offer of help could have been tokenistic but he came back to take up their case again and again. Then there were whistleblowers who came to give evidence or pass on documents and reports. The collective efforts of some of these individuals are represented in our play by our character *Fujitsu IT*.

As for the villains, that is a longer list than we have space to print but we suspect several spaces have been reserved for them in the long term parking bay of Hell. A fraction of them get a mention in our play. These depictions are satirical of course - in reality our portrayals will barely scratch the surface of all that was said and done by so many. What you see in our play is an overview of the scandal and how it impacted those it touched. If you want to know more, the detail is all out there to be found and you can follow the Public Inquiry on YouTube.

*"You can know anything. It's all there. You just have to find it."*

# COMPOSING THE SCORE FOR FALSE ACCOUNTS
## BY COMPOSER ICE DOB

I was kindly introduced to Lance by Chris Jones after composing a section of the score which featured in his film: 'Impact 50'. Our first meeting was a Zoom call on a hot summer day in which Lance and Suzette broke down the key features of the play and his vision for the score – I was immediately excited!

During this meeting, we finalised a list of all the music cues which would be needed for the production, which allowed me to brainstorm a few rough ideas before watching an initial run through.

This read through took place on a Zoom call, allowing me to mute my microphone and test various melodies on a piano whilst the actors spoke their lines. This was extremely useful as I was able to guage how long each section should be and which mood the music should be, in order to complement rather than detract from the acting. I then transferred some of these rough ideas into MIDI sequences on my laptop software to develop them further, searching through different synthesiser and virtual instrument sounds to try and find a suitable tone.

## Composing the Score for False Accounts

Lance and I had frequent meetings in which we would discuss the track ideas, and he would provide feedback on what he wanted to be altered for the final piece. This meant that the composition process was very collaborative and remained relevant to the overall piece throughout. I often composed multiple variations of a single music cue, consisting of either different melodies or instrument sounds, and therefore found Lance's input extremely helpful. When arranging the pieces, I tried to balance traditional phrasing with building the track based on the progression of the script. To achieve this, I recorded myself speaking the lines to create a rough guide and attempted to mirror the changes in pace and emotion melodically and rhythmically. Whilst this was not entirely accurate due to the nature of theatre, I found this process to be very effective, especially in maintaining the simplicity of the accompaniment as it allowed me to understand where space was necessary to enable the cast's performance to have its full impact.

My approach when it comes to composing varies heavily depending on which cue I am focussing on; during this project as a whole, I worked in a variety of different manners, sometimes approaching the track with a pre-existing idea for the melody, and other times scrolling through different instrumental sounds and experimenting until an idea presents itself. I think the most important aspect of composing, especially when working with deadlines, is to be persistent, as often a solution will manifest itself following enough trial and error.

The entire score was composed entirely on my laptop, using a combination of plug-ins to create the melodic elements. The majority of acoustic elements came from the BBC Symphony Orchestra Core collection by Spitfire Audio, which provides access to a host of different orchestral instruments and features interactive controls which adjust the way in which the sequence is played, which in turn creates a more realistic sound. I also used Omnisphere as the main source for my electronic elements, mainly due to the wide range of sounds it contains and the option to edit them in heavy detail (by layering different samples and even the level at which they can be heard).

I really enjoyed combining electronic and classical elements due to my background as both a DJ and percussionist. I also used the online database Splice to find suitable samples. Within my composition, I was inspired by Colin Stenson's combination of acoustic and electronic sounds within the 'Hereditary' soundtrack. This allowed homage to be paid to the fundamental classical roots of film scoring whilst similarly maintaining a modern sound. Furthermore, his use of dissonance and manipulation of audio (through his alteration of recorded saxophone sequences) also was very effective in creating tension.

Whilst 'False Accounts' did not require tension to be built to this extent, I found incorporating Stenson's harmonic techniques (such as the use of ostinatos and pedal notes) to suit the opening and interval tracks perfectly – as they both served to heighten tension and foreshadow upcoming events. Following Lance's recommendation, I was also inspired by the simplicity, beauty and authenticity of Carter Burwell's score for 'And The Band Played On', which perfectly heightens core emotions of each scene without overwhelming the listener or overshadowing the actors performing.

Furthermore, I took inspiration from Jerry Goldsmith's masterful use of dynamics and texture within his soundtrack for 'Alien' and attempted to mimic it by varying the volume and number of instruments playing at any one time. Equally, in terms of melodic development and the use of motifs, I tried to emulate elements from Jung Jae-Il's 'Parasite' score.

Overall, I had an amazing experience composing the score for the production, particularly due to the collaborative nature of the project and the opportunity to explore a host of different musical styles.

**Ice 'Dib' Dob - Composer of the score for False Accounts**

# TAKING ON THE STORY OF THE HORIZON POST OFFICE SCANDAL
## BY WRITER/CO-DIRECTOR LANCE STEEN ANTHONY NIELSEN

In 1997 I moved back to North London and lived just round the corner from a Post Office branch on Archway Road in N6. I've been a North Londoner ever since, and it will always be the place I call home as I've now lived most of my life there. Although much of my memory between 1997 and 2004 is a bit of a blank due to a tricky spell in hospital, one thing I do remember is the woman who ran my local Post Office.

She was a larger than life type of character and always cheerful. Her parents had emigrated to the UK from Pakistan and she was born and raised in the UK, and had been running the business for some years. She was a friendly chatty sort, and those kinds of people tend to stick in ones mind, especially when you're in the branch a couple of times a week.

When several Post Offices were shut down during a round of severe cuts to the service, the one on Archway Road was among them. I was one of many people who responded in protest to the survey about the 'proposed' closure. Post Office Limited was dismissive of our concerns, citing that people could just travel further to the nearest one in Highgate. This made me wonder why they bothered to send out the survey in the first place, when they clearly had every intention to close the branch regardless. It's funny how this sort of abstract mentality was a sign of things to come for what would turn out to be the biggest miscarriage of justice in British history.

Fast forward to 2010 and having picked up a newspaper on the London Underground I noticed a story about a Subpostmaster (the term for the owner of a Post Office branch) being convicted for theft. Her name was Seema Misra, and the way the narrative was being framed reminded me of how the press had scapegoated Social Worker Lisa Arthurworrey following the death of Victoria Climbie in Haringey. Seema was given a 15 month sentence for her criminal conviction. She was pregnant at the time when she went to prison.

Seeing Seema's picture, the first thing that struck me about her was that she was a dead ringer for the lady who ran the Archway Road branch. At first I thought Seema was the same person, prompting me to follow her story. It turned out Seema was not my old postmistress but my interest in the story was piqued. A short time later I read about a different Subpostmaster being prosecuted for false accounting. So I began to look into the story, and the seeds were sown of what would become twelve years become the play *False Accounts*.

This play went through several incarnations before finally becoming the production you're about to read, or indeed see on stage - hopefully both! My first idea was a two-hander set in a woman's prison, focusing on the relationship between two inmates, one of whom was to be based on Seema and her experience of injustice at the hands of Post Office Limited. But when I realised the scale of this was so much larger than just a couple of Subpostmasters, it transformed into *The Post Office Monologues*.

This second incarnation would have had six victims of the scandal telling their stories, cutting from one to the other on stage. This version would have gone ahead, but life intervened and the project was put on hold. Ultimately this type of play would have suffered by comparison with *The Vagina Monologues*, although mine was very different in tone. This delay was probably a blessing because over the next few years the true scale of the scandal became clear, and I realised the story required a different approach. For one thing, if I just told the story of the Subpostmasters we were really letting off the main culprits rather lightly.

Secondly, I felt the play as it stood, though powerful, was feeling a little dry. I wanted the audience to have the fullest possible picture of all that had transpired, but didn't want to do another Public Inquiry play. Even with inquiry into this travesty now fully underway, most people still haven't heard of The Post Office Scandal. Also, the best way to let a serious message land is to find a way to entertain your audience, telling them a story they want to remember, not one they quickly want to forget.

The play turning towards satire was largely down to two individuals. One was a former Subpostmaster who described the ineffectiveness of the National Federation of Subpostmasters (Their union in all but name) being down to their elected board *'Having their noses in the trough for far too long'*. Soon afterwards I wrote the scene where the Federation was depicted in this fashion and could tell that it was going to work. Secondly Ian Henderson's description of the people he met at Fujitsu as being *'A right bunch of Muppets'* gave me another idea which could convey these sentiments rather strongly.

I've always been interested in using music and sound design in my stage productions and I brought in an incredibly talented computer in the form of Ice Dob (or Ice 'Dib' Dob, as I call them) to give the production an emotional backbone that you'd normally only get in a film. I know not everyone likes music in theatre productions that are non-musical in nature, but fusing elements of Theatre and Cinema has always been something I've pushed in my shows and it's incredibly effective here.

I also need to give a nod to a play which inspired me to try something new with my next production - that was the Young Vic's production of *A Season In The Congo* which used extremely clever techniques, including puppets, to convey a very serious historical story. It was, and still is, one of the best plays I've ever seen (and my good friend Sharon Duncan Brewster was in it!).

One final twist in the tale was that two members of The Outcasts Creative had actually worked for the Horizon Helpline and Post Office Limited respectively during the height of the scandal coming to light. Another individual also had access to un-redacted minutes of secret committee meetings within the Post Office. The cat was truly out the bag when I got my hands on those.

So in 2019 I began to work on what would be the third version for the play which premiered in October 2022 at The Old Joint Stock Theatre in Birmingham and then in November at The Questors Theatre in London. The script went through numerous cuts and edits, even during the Birmingham and London runs. Some scenes and characters had to go and I was constantly re-shaping it. The cast also contributed towards the development of the production, bringing some of the characters to life in a way that only actors can do, putting their own stamp on different segments. It was a great collective experience produced with meagre resources.

Our budget for the production was minimal but we did have several individuals who stepped up to cover costs until they could be reimbursed. To that end I am especially indebted to Claire and Billy George, friends I had not seen for many years whose support for our show was unparalleled.

I've done several unfunded and low/no budget plays in my lifetime but I was adamant that last years production of False Accounts would be the last I'd undertake. The main reason for this decision was that at this stage in my career, I feel very strongly I should not be having to ask actors to do a play for profit share. I should be in the position to offer those actors that have supported my work in the past, paid work on future projects. Not being able to do this is, and has been, incredibly frustrating. As I have got older I've come to realise that the funding system isn't really there to help people like me in the Arts.

Sure you can applying for funding and try and stand out among thousands of applicants, but there doesn't seem to be anyone who actually looks at the track record of a creative who has been consistently doing unfunded output to a high standard. Someone like myself telling stories like this, against all the odds, who might actually say 'hey we should help this person you know, look at all they've achieved without any proper funding...'

I thought when I started out it would work that way for my career, but it hasn't, sadly, such is the competitive nature of our industry. Sometimes, to get where you want to be, you have to do it by sheer force of will. Believe me, I've been trying. To keep this in perspective, I have been beavering away at this full time since 1997. In the last two decades I've applied for all kinds of funding, grants and writing positions with prestigious theatre venues, and continued to create my own output when no external support was forthcoming. I've won a few awards, had some good notices, and got Time Out's Critics Choice (twice), but that doesn't seem to mean anything these days.

At the last venue of note where I applied for a position, they were taking on four new writers to develop in house. I called the venue to check if they would be interested in someone my age, or if it was just about finding the next hot young talent. I was assured they were looking for writers of all ages across the board. As part of the application you had to have a reference from someone who worked in the industry, saying why you would be an asset to that theatre. I had four, three of them from established actors who had performed on their stage. Despite this, I still didn't even get shortlisted for an interview.

During lockdown, I applied for several positions and competitions. One, which a prestigious multi award-winning director had put his name to, was all about discovering new writing talent for television and feature films. It sounded promising and again I put in the work as the application was complex. I applied for four different rounds of varying genres, but every time I was due to get the promised confirmation of my application, I had to chase for one, whereas fellow applicants always got their notifications on time. I thought it was just a glitch, but when they didn't even bother to send me the proper rejection email, but following my inquiry re-directed me to the link page where it was supposed to be sent from, (which literally had a section that said 'insert name of applicant here') I think it is fair to say my application hadn't even been looked at. You also had to include a two minute video of yourself. It was evident these were more important for selection than the quality of the actual story you were submitting.

Don't get me wrong, I've had a ton of rejections, but these last couple had a different impact. They made me feel that at my age I no longer had anything to offer this industry. After nearly three decades of trying to get funding for projects, I'd come as far as I was going to get on my own, so I thought independent productions and I had finally departed ways. Getting funding for anything creative is incredibly difficult, carving out a career without any support from the pillars of the industry is even more so. I've given my whole life to the Creative Arts and it also cost me the most important person in my life. I don't plan to leave the industry entirely. I am just shifting my focus towards things that make me happy - my YouTube channel, publishing all of my scripts and plays, writing the rest of my Science Fiction novel series and my work as an acting coach. The best way people can show support for my change in direction is by purchasing my plays and novels from Amazon and subscribing to my YouTube channel and watching its content.

With all that said, this story, as important as it was, enticed me back to take on one more show.

I came to this production with an extremely difficult 24 months behind me, so taking on the huge responsibility that this story deserved was more than a little bit daunting at the time. But to be honest, diving into this play in 2022 probably saved both my life and my sanity. So I actually feel as though I owe the Subpostmasters a huge debt, because without them there would be no story for me to tell. The 2022 production gave me a focus I really needed, allowing time for some really deep personal wounds to heal.

Life can be like that sometimes - it works in ways you don't expect. Furthermore the former Subpostmasters came in large numbers to see the production. Not really knowing what to expect they embraced my approach to telling their story and their support for our efforts was beyond measure.

The line between telling an emotionally complex and deeply personal story and taking a satirical approach is an extremely tight one to navigate, but I was confident it would work if done correctly and with the passion the story deserved. The praise the victims of the scandal gave the production was the only affirmation that mattered to me. Sure, positive reviews are nice, but the story we were telling belonged to the former Subpostmasters. Fortunately the audiences loved it too. I always make a point of talking to as many people as I can as they leave the venue, asking them what they thought of the show. The response from all that I spoke to was universally positive.

One of the high points for me personally was on the opening night in Birmingham. I was backstage with Birmingham Producer / Stage Manager Suzette Pluck as actor Graham McDonald was going full throttle on stage with one of his first Fujitsu IT speeches, and we whispered 'Christ we did it - we got it on!' We smiled and had a big hug knowing we'd reached a milestone most would have thought impossible. It was a huge achievement for us all that the production was up and running and more importantly it appeared to be working.

The 2022 run of the show was not without its hiccups. When people are on profit share and more lucrative job offers come along actors have to take them, and we lost two cast members with only a week to go. So there was much frantic running around to get the replacement cast members up to speed. Some actors went on stage with the minimum level of rehearsal.

Then literally three days before the opening night of the Birmingham show, one of our cast was rushed into hospital with a collapsed lung. Not wanting to put anyone else in the cast under additional pressure by having them read in for another part at such short notice, I took on one of their main roles and Outcasts regular Sebastian Storey came in to take on the roles of Auditor 2 and Gareth Jenkins.

Prior to the performance a short announcement was made that an understudy would be on stage with a script and at one point I was having so much fun playing this additional role that I shut my script in glee and totally lost my place. I stayed in character and ad libbed until I found my place again. Such is the joy of theatre - as the great Dame Judi Dench said *'You never know what to expect from one performance to the next, every night is different and that is what makes it such fun.'*

Big established venues with well funded shows rarely have to deal with such issues, and casts will have a minimum of three weeks rehearsal with all the company working in the same space. On the 2022 production we only had three days in the actual space, with the rest of our rehearsals all being online. The fact that we were able to pull the production off was a testament to the skill and commitment of the cast and our determination as a company to see the production through.

Birmingham had a company of 12 actors, London had a larger cast of 14 to allow more students of *The Outcasts Creative* Monday night acting class to take part. This gave one of our students his first real crack at an acting role. Shaz Ali, whom Dickon and I could not be more proud of, would subsequently be cast in the second play about the Grenfell inquiry, Grenfell System Failure. Our 2023 production brings the cast down to ten, which will make it a very intense show indeed, and I can't wait to see how it shapes up.

Our proudest moment as a company in 2022 was the last night in London. We had a full house and I made the impulsive decision to call all the former Subpostmasters in the audience to come onto the stage and take a the final bow with the company, as well as the Birmingham cast present that evening. Only Rosanna Preston was sadly missing at the time. Kevin Brown (whom I have asked to write the forward for this publication) put his arm around me and thanked us for all that we had done on their behalf. He said among other things:

*'We thought we had been forgotten, but you proved there are still decent people out there. You've restored our faith.'*

I cannot recall the rest of his words but it took every ounce of strength I had not to burst into tears on the stage. There is a photograph of this moment taken by Journalist Nick Wallace with my co-director and co-founder of the Outcasts, Dickon Tolson standing behind me, looking as if he too is about to weep. It was one of the proudest moments of my career. The fact that it meant so much to them, is what meant so much to us all. It's not lost on me that we're a small theatre company, telling a massive story that really deserves to be on stage at somewhere like the National Theatre. We had no funding and we did it anyway, in no small part thanks to all the people mentioned in the pages of this book. I'll be giving this production the biggest push that I can to get it into a West End Theatre, because if I can do that, I know the story of what happened to these people will get tremendous momentum.

I've made the personal decision to pull away from production at the end of 2023. However, as I have told our company - I can't recall a story more deserving of success than this one, and its arrival on stage could not be more timely. If we can reach our ultimate goal one day, then the company will certainly have earned it. We're a production team of only thirteen people this time around, but never before have I seen a company work so hard towards a common goal. Everyone mucking in, doing extra jobs where required, taking on extra rehearsals with little complaint, and at this stage, all for just the meagre financial rewards of a profit share production. They are truly an outstanding company. While the rewards of a West End transfer would be symbiotic for all concerned, I know I can speak for everyone to say nothing would make us happier than to be able to tell this tale to the widest audience possible. Only yesterday with the OSO production just two weeks away, we've already confirmed a transfer to the prestigious Gatehouse Theatre in Highgate for a further week from the 20-25th of June 2023. So I am happy to say that our production is already gaining some much deserved momentum.

So, if this play turns out to be my last, I will certainly have ended my two decade run of shows with one of the most important travesties of justice in our country's history. Not a bad note to got out with. Or is it just the end of the beginning for this play? Time will tell.

**Lance Steen Anthony Nielsen - May 2023**

PS - *Please do Subscribe to The Outcasts Creative channel on YouTube, and if you have a Creative project you would like us to talk about on there, please do get in touch.*

# CAST & CREW OF THE 2022 & 2023 PRODUCTIONS OF FALSE ACCOUNTS

### OSO Arts Centre / The Gatehouse Theatre 2023 Cast (10)

*The cast for the London OSO Theatre, Barnes, 2023 production are played by an ensemble of ten actors playing the following roles:*

**Katheryn Siggers** - Narrator / Villager 2 / Reviewer 2 / Fed 3 / Helpline 2 / Susan Crichton

**Miriam Babooram** - Postmaster 1 / Fujitsu Muppet 1

**Victoria Jeffrey** - Postmaster 2 / Reviewer 3 / Alice Perkins

**Dickon Tolson** - Postmaster 3 / Fed 1 / Ian Henderson

**Ali Zaidi** - Postmaster 5 / Fujitsu Boss / Boeing Manager

**Maggie Robson\*** - Paula Vennells / Mrs Bates / Horizon Trainer / Villager 1 / Mr Piggerton (Fed 4) / Helpline 3

**Alex Heaton** - Auditor 1 / Chris Aujard / Villager 3 / John Scott

**Dave Binder** - Auditor 2 / Fed 5 / Gareth Jenkins / Belinda Crowe / Max Penalty

*Cast & Crew of the 2022 & 2023 Productions of False Accounts*

**Francesca Marago** - The Gatekeeper / Villager 4 / Gina / Fujitsu IT / Fed 2 / Helpline 1 / Alwen Lyons / Fujitsu Muppet 2

**Donna Combe** - Postmaster 4/4B / Reviewer 1 / Angela Van Den Bogerd

**Gary Boulter** (Outcasts Australia) - Voice of the Judge

———

(Cover) **Rosamund Carpenter** - Mr Piggerton / Horizon Trainer / Helpline

(Cover) **Gill Broderick*** - Paula Vennells / villager 1 / Reviewer 3

(Cover) **Marta Fossati** - Assistant of John Scott

* At the time of publication the roles of Maggie Robson for the OSO production are being covered by Rosamund Carpenter and Gillian Broderick

———

The 2022 Birmingham production had twelve, and London had fourteen in the company. A breakdown of the cast for both companies is as follows:

**Birmingham Old Joint Stock Theatre - 2022 Cast (12)**

**Aila Swan** - Narrator / Susan Crichton / Villager / Helpline

**Balbir Rallmil** - Postmaster 1

**Rosanna Preston** - Postmaster 2 / Alice Perkins / Reviewer

**Alan Wales** - Postmaster 3 / Ian Henderson / Fed Chairman

**Cathy Odusanya** - Postmaster 4

**William Hayes** - Postmaster 5 / Boeing & Fujitsu Manager

**Graham McDonald** - Fujitsu IT/Max Penalty/Fed/Belinda Crowe

*Cast & Crew of the 2022 & 2023 Productions of False Accounts*

**Alex Heaton** - Auditor 1 / Villager / Chris Aujard

**Kenny O'Connor** - Auditor 2 / Chris Aujard / Gareth Jenkins

**Elaine Ward** - Paula Vennells / Horizon Trainer / Mr Piggerton

**Tara Lacey** - Gatekeeper/Villager/Fed/Helpline/Alwen Lyons

**Gary Boulter** (Outcasts Australia) - Voice of the Judge

(Cover) **Sarah Pitts** - Angela Van Den Bogerd / Mrs Bates

(Cover) **Sebastian Storey** - Auditor 2 / Gareth Jenkins

*All other roles played by various members of the company*

---

**London Questors Theatre Ealing - 2022 Cast (14)**

**Anne Hayward** - Narrator / Villager

**Jasmina Zaveri** - Postmaster 1

**Theresa Cole** - Postmaster 2 / Alwen Lyons

**Dickon Tolson** - Postmaster 3 / Ian Henderson

**Cathy Odusanya** - Postmaster 4 / 4B

**William Hayes** - Postmaster 5/Boeing & Fujitsu Managers

**Shaz Ali** - Fujitsu IT

**Graham McDonald** - Max Penalty/Fed/Belinda Crowe

**Alex Heaton** - Auditor 1 / Villager / Judge

**Kenny O'Connor** - Auditor 2/Chris Aujard/Gareth Jenkins

**Maggie Robson** - Paula Vennells/Horizon Trainer/Mr Piggerton

**Edward Glennie** - Fed Chairman/Helpline/Angela Van Den Bogerd

**Tara Lacey** - Alwen Lyons/Gatekeeper/Villager/Fed/Helpline

*Cast & Crew of the 2022 & 2023 Productions of False Accounts*

**Bella Jacob** - Susan Crichton/Villager/Reviewer

*All other roles played by various members of the company*

---

**Production Team 2022 & 2023**

**Produced and Directed** by Dickon Tolson & Lance Steen Anthony Nielsen

**Producers** - Billy George, Suzette Pluck, Lance Steen Anthony Nielsen & Dickon Tolson (2022) - Victoria Jeffrey, Lance Steen Anthony Nielsen & Dickon Tolson (2023)

**Social Media, Photography & Videos by** - Francesca Marago & Katheryn Siggers (2023)

**Music composed** by Ice Dob

**Assistant Director** - Marta Fossati (2023)

**Stage Managers** - Suzette Pluck (2022) Marta Fossati (2023)

**Assistant Stage Manager** - Rosamund Bev Carpenter (2023)

**Technicians** - Roni Elson & Erica Talbott-Morgan (Birmingham 2022) Jonny Danciger (2023 - OSO Theatre) Lou-Lila Masson-Lacroix (2023 - The Gatehouse, Highgate)

**Production Design Consultant** - Chris de Wilde

**Poster and Programme Design** - Anne Hayward

**Puppetry Consultant** - Melissa Stanton

# BREAKING DOWN THE ROLES

*As with any story based on historical events and actual people, certain physical casting requirements for some roles warrant a mention here. Most of the Subpostmasters are based on amalgamations of two to three real people who were victims of the scandal. Consequently they have definitive gender and ethnicity characteristics which tie into the broad facts of their story. However the racial make-up of the cast can be swapped around and is flexible, with the exception of Postmaster 1 who has a very specific storyline. Postmaster 4 has been both of African & Scottish heritage in different productions and Postmaster 5 has been both caucasian and Asian. The key is that they're the outsider who doesn't become connected to the others until the High Court case.*

*Postmaster 1 is a female over 40 of Asian/Indian appearance.*

*Postmaster 2 is a white female over the age of 50.*

*Postmaster 3 is a male, late 40s+, from the North East of England.*

*Postmaster 4 is female, 40+, any ethnicity / background.*

*Postmaster 5 is male, 40+, any ethnicity / background.*

*In the same context, the characters of the Sparrow Committee should be cast with white/caucasian actors if possible. (Actors 6, 7, 8, & 9) Although the play is a satire, the racial make up of this group is actually quite important to the truth of the story.*

*In the 2023 production the ensemble cast of ten actors portrayed a number of roles between them, which were divided as follows:*

ACTOR 1 – Narrator / Villager 2 / Reviewer 2 / Fed 3 / Helpline 2 / Susan Crichton

ACTOR 2 – Postmaster 1 / Angela VDB / Fujitsu Muppet 1

ACTOR 3 – Postmaster 2 / Reviewer 3 / Alice Perkins

ACTOR 4 – Postmaster 3 / Fed 1 / Ian Henderson

ACTOR 5 – Postmaster 5 / Fujitsu Boss / Boeing Manager / John Scott

ACTOR 6 – Paula Vennells / Mrs Bates / Horizon Trainer / Villager 1 / Fed 4 (Mr Piggerton) / Helpline 3

ACTOR 7 – Auditor 1 / Chris Aujard / Villager 3

ACTOR 8 – Auditor 2 / Fed 5 / Gareth Jenkins / Belinda Crowe / Max Penalty

ACTOR 9 – The Gatekeeper / Villager 4 / Gina / Fujitsu IT / Fed 2 / Helpline 1 / Alwen Lyons / Fujitsu Muppet 2

ACTOR 10 – Postmaster 4 / 4B / Reviewer 1

*The company play additional villagers and Federation members if required. Depending on casting Angela Van Den Bogerd can be played by either Actor 2 or Actor 10.*

# 1

# ACT I - FALSE ACCOUNTS

*The play has been broken down into a series of named and numbered scenes for the purpose of rehearsals.*

*A single table sits in the space, rear stage centre, with three chairs either side. On the table sits a model of a set, covered with a red cloth.*

*AUDITORS 1 & 2 are preset in the space. The two characters are dressed in long, light coloured coats and flat caps.*

*HOUSE OPEN – MUSIC CUE SQ 1. (15 minute track, main theme for the show)*

*As the audience enter THE AUDITORS roam the space, greeting them and inquiring as to the costs of their clothes, travel to the venue, whether they have purchased any expensive holidays in recent times etc etc.*

*Upon clearance ACTOR 9, planted in the audience, stands and addresses the house, reading the disclaimer (below).*

**LEGAL DISCLAIMER** - Welcome to this evening's performance of False Accounts. The following production is based on a true story; however many events have been condensed for simplicity and dramatic purposes. But much of what you will see and hear allegedly happened. Although many names and facts will be presented with the greatest accuracy, the narrative of the story and portrayal of characters must be viewed in a satirical context, and is not intended to be an accurate depiction of any individual. Allegedly.

*When the NARRATOR ENTERS below, that is their cue to EXIT.*

*1) OPENING*

*MUSIC CUE – TRACK SQ 2.*

*NARRATOR ENTERS – walks to centre stage (aged between 20-30, either gender).*

**NARRATOR** – Computers. Gotta love them. We've all got one. There's one in almost every home, there's one in every phone. Switched off I hope? Good. Just checking. They're designed to make our lives easier, more expedient and efficient. But when they go wrong, they can cause great harm, or even worse, kill people. A bug in the computer software designed to run the new Boeing MAX 737 aircraft, MCAS, had a nasty flaw. Under certain circumstances it could abruptly order a plane into a steep dive, giving even the most experienced of pilots about 40 seconds to diagnose the error and recover their aircraft. The pilots of Lion Air Flight 610 could not save theirs. So 189 people were gone. The lives of their loved ones, torn apart. Just like that. Because of a computer error the designers failed to spot.

*BOEING MANAGER ENTERS – (40s, white shirt and tie, American accent). The NARRATOR glares upon their arrival.*

**NARRATOR** - After the first crash of flight 610, if just one person in a key position of authority at Boeing had stood up and said –

**BOEING MANAGER** – 'We've got to ground those planes right now and solve this problem! Otherwise there is a real threat to passenger safety here!'

**NARRATOR** – Then those 157 souls of Ethiopian flight 302, which crashed 5 months later, would still be alive today. But no one spoke up, so they were killed. Even after that second crash, Boeing still wouldn't ground their new MAX fleet, seeking to blame the pilots...

**BOEING MANAGER** - There is nothing wrong with MCAS! I mean - Lion and Ethiopian airways. We're dealing with third world countries here. I doubt their pilots were up to our standards. We're not grounding those planes! Do you have an idea how much that would cost? No sir. Our planes are staying in the air!

**NARRATOR** – You know who grounded those planes, causing the rest of the world to follow suit? China. I know, right? Placing blind faith in a computer system you believe to be absolutely infallible can cost lives.

*The pair exchange a glare. BOEING MANAGER exits.*

**NARRATOR** – At the turn of the new millennium, another new computer system called Horizon would be installed in every Post Office across the United Kingdom. Horizon was overdue, over budget, and full of bugs, and many of the Subpostmasters did not welcome its arrival. But they had no choice but to give up the old way of doing things and embrace the new technology. So the scene was set for what would become the biggest miscarriage of justice in British history.

*SQ 2 FADES OUT INTO SQ 3.*

*NARRATOR pulls off the cloth revealing the model of a Post Office set & EXITS.*

**2) AUDITORS INTRO**

*MUSIC CUE SQ 3– AUDITORS THEME (Paused half way in).*

*AUDITORS 1 & 2 ENTER – (40+ long coats, shirt and ties).*

**AUDITOR 1** – We are the Post Office Auditing team. Right sir?

**AUDITOR 2** – We are indeed sir. If your branch books don't balance, or if you're getting regular shortfalls...

**AUDITOR 1** – Or if you have discrepancies that you cannot account for...

**AUDITOR 2** – Then you can expect a visit from us to your branch.

**AUDITOR 1** – And if you or your staff have got sticky fingers then we will know sir!

**AUDITOR 2** – That's right sir. And if we catch you, we will use a proceeds of crime order to take every single thing you own! So if we have to visit you, then...

**AUDITOR 1** (Pointing to model interrupting) – Sorry to interrupt your opening monologue sir - what is that?

**AUDITOR 2** – What? This sir?

**AUDITOR 1** – Yes, that miniature house thing on the stage sir.

**AUDITOR 2** – That is a physical representation, vis a vis, model of our set sir.

**AUDITOR 1** (looking around the stage) – It doesn't look much like our set sir? In fact it looks much nicer than our set. (looking around) Why don't we have a set like that sir?

**AUDITOR 2** – Unfortunately this model of our proposed set design only arrived today. So there wasn't enough time or money for us to build the actual set sir.

**AUDITOR 1** – So if we're not going to use it, what's it doing on the stage then sir?

**AUDITOR 2** (pointing to the model) – This is there to represent something else sir. It's what you call an 'anagram...'

**AUDITOR 1** – An Anagram sir?

AUDITOR 2 – Yes sir. It means when a thing stands in for another thing to represent a different thing.

AUDITOR 1 – Ahhhhh, you mean a metaphor sir?

AUDITOR 2 – Right, a matador, that's what I meant. So think of this model as being a representation of Horizon.

AUDITOR 1 – Horizon? Do you mean the amazingly robust computer system installed in every Post Office across the country that could never, ever, be in error sir?

AUDITOR 2 – The one and the same sir. Imagine in this case, it is standing in for the prototype design of the Horizon program.

AUDITOR 1 – Right... I am imagining very hard and it don't like much a computer to me sir.

AUDITOR 2 – Ahhh yes sir. This is where the matador comes in.

AUDITOR 1 - Metaphor.

AUDITOR 2 – Right, that's what I said. So, when you design a computer software that's going to run terminals in Post Offices all over the country, what you do is build a smaller prototype first, to see if it works, like this is a smaller prototype of our set. So let's say this model 'as a metaphor' now represents the initial design of the new Horizon system from Fujitsu.

AUDITOR 1 – Foowho now?

AUDITOR 2 – Fujitsu. They were contracted to design Horizon for the Post Office. Now imagine if they designed this tiny prototype but then ran out of time. So instead of going away and constructing the larger system required to run the transactions for every Post Office branch in the country, they just ran with this smaller prototype version instead...

AUDITOR 1 – I'm not a technical man you understand. But I feel that might not work too well sir.

**AUDITOR 2** – It did not sir. But that's exactly what they decided to do...

SQ 4 - MUSIC CUE – AUDITORS THEME EXIT (second half).

COMPANY (minus the two Auditors) ENTER, dressed as various VILLAGERS / POSTMASTERS 2, 3, 4 & 5.

### 3) THE VILLAGE OF BUCKFORD / POSTMASTERS INTRO

SQ 5 - MUSIC CUE – Peer Gynt – Morning Mood (start 30 seconds in).

Three of the chairs are placed downstage left to form a bench.

POSTMASTER 1 ENTERS LAST – (40+, female, smart casual attire). She takes centre stage, smiling at the audience. As they speak the VILLAGERS walk past smiling, two of them play cricket, etc, choreography to be worked out for each character. (Several of the villagers will also become Postmaster characters in this sequence) There's a Postman, a Butcher wearing an apron, another is fishing, someone else sits and does the newspaper crossword etc.

VILLAGER 3 crosses stage and sits on the bench, which is the cue for PM 1 to speak.

**POSTMASTER 1** – 1999, such a different time. The information super highway was only just becoming a thing. That's what we called the internet in those days. There wasn't any social media to preoccupy everyone's time and only a handful of us actually had mobile phones. You couldn't dump your soon-to-be ex by text. Dating apps weren't even a thing, let alone chatrooms, people still had actual conversations in person, especially in little villages like this. We'd lived in the city for years and my husband and I were wanting a change, so when we heard the Subpostmaster of this rural branch near my Mum's was selling up, it felt like the perfect business we were looking for. I loved that village, so the transition all felt so natural for us really.

SQ 6 - MUSIC fades out slowly during speech.

**POSTMASTER 1** - The Post Office is the beating heart of any small community and when you're manning the desk every day you get to know everyone in the village pretty quickly. They all said hello and even smiled at us in the street. Oh, hello...

**VILLAGER 1** – How are you settling in?

**POSTMASTER 1** – Just fine thank you Reg/Regina. We absolutely love it here.

**VILLAGER 1** – Glad to hear it, I'm running a movie quiz down the pub this Friday, hope to see you there.

**POSTMASTER 1** – You can count on it. (to audience) We were soon regulars at the pub quiz, watched the cricket playing on the green every Sunday. We all knew each other's names. Morning George.... (Or female name)

**VILLAGER 2** – Morning Mrs Jackson....

**POSTMASTER 1** – It's Mrs Smith. Anyway, we sold everything from television licences to fishing permits, travellers cheques to lottery tickets. Every week we had our regulars and they always liked a bit of a chat.

*VILLAGER 2 approaches and is given their lottery tickets.*

**VILLAGER 2** – Did you see that couple that won the Euro last week? They'd only just bought themselves a five bedroom house and already own a couple of ponies, and then they go and win one hundred million quid! People like that shouldn't be allowed to play the Lotto if you ask me!

*VILLAGER 3 approaches the counter, with their lottery ticket.*

**POSTMASTER 1** – You never know, it could be you! (to audience) People loved moaning about not winning the lottery. And the size of their gas and electric bills. Something tells me that's not going to change. But most of all they just loved to talk to you. Sometimes it would be about the weather.

**VILLAGER 3** – I think it looks like rain today... don't you? Probably rain again tomorrow. They say its going to rain this weekend. I bet it's going to rain next week. Didn't we talk about the rain last week?

**POSTMASTER 1** – Yes, we did. Other times they'd want to tell you the latest gossip.

**VILLAGER 4** – I heard he ran off with the new girl they'd hired behind the bar. I mean honestly, taking on a twenty year old Filipino with a chest the size of Everest is just asking for trouble isn't it? That's a mountain by the way... Everest.

**POSTMASTER 1** – You don't say. For the most part people were lovely. Anyway, we soon got the hang of running the branch, but I have to admit I liked the old way of doing things. I had a good head for figures and if we had a shortfall you could easily check your paperwork and you'd find the problem.

*One of the VILLAGERS now becomes POSTMASTER 2.*

**POSTMASTER 2** – We'd all called it 'The Royal Mail' for so long, you always felt The Post Office was a trusted brand with this almost regal quality. I'd worked for them ever since I left school at 17. First behind the counter, then later my Subpostmistress made me her Deputy Manager. It was great having some responsibility for the first time in my life. My Mother told me how proud she was of me, because at school I wasn't exactly top of the class. But as my Dad said, I was a grafter and I knew how to knuckle down and work hard. So I decided one day I was going to run a branch of my own. For two decades, we never had any problems.

*One of the VILLAGERS becomes POSTMASTER 3, one VILLAGER is GINA.*

**POSTMASTER 3** – Evening all, how are you? I like being married. Twenty five years next week. I'll Never forget the first time I laid my eyes on our Gina. It was time to show my dance skills, so I had a word with the DJ!

*SQ 7 - MUSIC CUE – Can't touch this – MC Hammer.*

*The VILLAGERS all briefly become CLUBBERS. POSTMASTER 3 does his dancing Dad number towards his wife-to-be GINA. (VILLAGER strips off their coat to reveal sparkly dress) The Old Man (VILLAGER 3) dances with GINA, but is soon cut in by POSTMASTER 3.*

**POSTMASTER 3** – Yeah the DJ hit MC Hammer, and I had those trousers on, put on some of my moves. (they do the MC Hammer dance in their cricket pads) She just melted into my arms, naturally. I knew there and then, this was the woman I was going to spend the rest of my life with.

*SQ 8 - MUSIC STOPS.*

*POSTMASTER 3 is passed two babies (dolls) by GINA, wrapped in blankets.*

**POSTMASTER 3** - The next thing you know I've got two kids and I'm about to become a grandfather. I know what you're thinking, he's too young. Ah what can I say, it's in the genes. You should see my kids, both good looking buggers an all.

*They hand the babies back to GINA who EXITS.*

**POSTMASTER 3** - Anyway, the Post Office branch we took over in 1995 was in a right state to be honest, but we both mucked in, spent about three hundred grand on renovations and modernised the whole thing. We rented out the upstairs flat and lived about 20 minutes away up the A41. There were never any issues and we ticked along quite nicely. We loved that part of world, and my big hobby was cricket. I played on the local team, well it was a good excuse to have a pint. Sipping a beer after a game on those warm summer nights were really the best of times.

*VILLAGER folds over their newspaper and becomes POSTMASTER 5 (45+, male).*

*OTHER VILLAGERS & POSTMASTERS EXIT (EXCEPT 4 & 2, 5).*

**POSTMASTER 5** – A trusted brand, guaranteed footfall through the doors and a small salary. As a business proposition it felt like a no-brainer to me. Back then you had a basic wage, but the real profit was to be found in the retail side of the business. Sure, some branches were closing, but I knew with my background in IT and sales experience, I could make a success of of the place, and so it was. Before the installation of Horizon, let me tell you something, if we had a shortfall I always found it. I was meticulously organised with my paperwork. Just ask my wife.

**MRS BATES** – (possibly off stage) He organises his DVD collection in alphabetical order, and by genre. God forbid I should put one back in the wrong place!

*POSTMASTER 5 produces a contract which they begin to peruse.*

**POSTMASTER 5** – (to the wings) Don't be leaving 'The Professionals' DVD discs next to the telly, put them back in the box, in the crime section sub-section, under television drama! (to the audience) She loves that Lewis Collins, I'm more of a Martin Shaw man myself. Now where was I? It might surprise you to learn that as a Subpostmaster I do not actually work for Post Office Ltd, or POL as most people call it these days. We're self-employed traders, and you're supposed to sign a contract and even the official secrets act before you take on a branch. As I found out later, getting to even see a contract could be down to pure chance, but I made sure I got hold of one and read every single line, twice. Buried in the pages I noticed a rather interesting clause.

*One of the VILLAGERS becomes POSTMASTER 4 (40+, either gender, any ethnicity) taking the contract from Postmaster 5.*

**POSTMASTER 4** – Subpostmasters Contract, Clause 12 of Section 12.... Ah yes, here we go – 'The Subpostmaster is responsible for all losses caused through his own negligence, carelessness or error, and also for losses of all kinds. Assistants Deficiencies due to such losses must be made good without delay.' I have to admit when I took on my branch I can't remember reading that at the time, and if I did, I certainly didn't appreciate what it meant. Basically any money that went missing was entirely your responsibility to make up. Before Horizon came along, the books always balanced and we never had any issues. I really enjoyed the job, I got to meet all types of people and the job was never boring. The installation of Horizon came about a year later, so I was sent off to Maidstone for three days training, the last of which took place back in my branch.

### 4) HORIZON TRAINING

*HORIZON TRAINER ENTERS – the model is turned to become the Horizon machine (prop) PM 4, 2 & 5 sit.*

**HORIZON TRAINER** – As you can see Horizon handles everything from the lottery, to stamps and benefits and all your retail items. So just like before, you balance everything on Wednesday, sign off the worksheet and send it off to Chesterfield. Easy peasey lemon squeezy.

**POSTMASTER 4** – So once I've done the weekly balance, if there is any kind of error, how do I go back and review transactions on the system?

**HORIZON TRAINER** – Error? I'm sorry, I don't follow you.

**POSTMASTER 4** –Well say there's some discrepancies or a maybe shortfall?

**HORIZON TRAINER** – Why would there be discrepancies? Oh I see, you mean if you've made a mistake!

**POSTMASTER 4** – No I mean if the computer makes a mistake. If Horizon goes wrong somehow?

**HORIZON TRAINER** – I'm sorry, I don't quite follow. How would it go wrong?

**POSTMASTER 4** – Because it's a computer and computers can malfunction.

**HORIZON TRAINER** – This is Horizon, it's very robust system you see. It doesn't go wrong.

*POSTMASTER 4 EXITS.*

**POSTMASTER 5** – (To audience) We heard that word a lot when it came to Horizon. 'Robust'. (To Trainer) It may well be robust, but if I get a transaction correction or a discrepancy, I need to be able to check to see where the error has occurred. How do I do that?

**HORIZON TRAINER** – If that has happened I think it's more likely you'll be having someone with light fingers in the branch. Or you might have input something incorrectly.

**POSTMASTER 5** – Right, so if I accidentally enter something twice, or for some reason the system goes down your end, all the sales will still go through completely correctly and balance out, will they?

**HORIZON TRAINER** – Erm.... yes. Probably. Horizon is very robust.

*POSTMASTER 5 EXITS.*

*The conversation continues with POSTMASTER 2.*

**POSTMASTER 2** – Robust, yes you said that already. So now we've finished adding everything for this training session, all the figures will balance correctly?

**HORIZON TRAINER** – Exactly. Just press that button there and hey presto.

*POSTMASTER 2 duly complies.*

**POSTMASTER 2** – Its not balanced, in fact it's down by £500...

**HORIZON TRAINER** – Impossible. I'm sure we did everything correctly. Let me see that. Ah, Right. Sometimes that happens. It's normally a terminal teething thing.

**POSTMASTER 2** – Terminal teething? Is that a technical term is it? I'm £500 quid down now and I haven't even opened yet!

**HORIZON TRAINER** – Yes don't worry about that, I'm sure it will sort itself out tomorrow.

*HORIZON TRAINER EXITS.*

**POSTMASTER 2** – It will sort itself out tomorrow - If I had a tenner for every time someone connected to Horizon told me that, I'd have 960 quid. Which would have come in handy, as now I had to pay that £500 out of my own pocket to cover that cock-up caused by the bloody trainer! I'm not joking, this really happened. After that we went from having books which balanced to one discrepancy, after another and the shortfall just got bigger and bigger. I don't really know computers, but it felt from the very beginning as if something with the design wasn't working properly.

*POSTMASTER 2 EXITS.*

### 5) WORKING FOR FUJITSU

*FUJITSU IT ENTERS – either gender, any age, wearing flip-flops, shades, loud shirt, messy hair.*

**FUJITSU IT** – Alright, yeah here with my peeps. Safe. I'm just your typical software code developer for Information Technology. I put the 'I' in the 'I-T', if you know what I mean bruv. Horizon... (laughs) Sure, I worked on it. If you think back to the months leading up to the new millennium with all that bollocks about Y2K, it was a time of real chancers for our industry. It was, and still is, full of people who don't really know what they were doing. You heard that phrase 'A bad workman blames his tools'? – that applies in IT. For most of you, IT probably feels like something very removed from your daily life - that's okay, I mean I can't fix a broken tap either. The story here really starts with Fujitsu, the company that won the contract to design the new software system that would run every Post Office in the country. Our coding team was based on this shitty industrial estate in darkest Bracknell. A town famous its number of roundabouts that really has fuck all else to recommend it, believe me. When I arrived at Fujitsu, the design team was somewhat lacking in leadership and they were already months behind schedule, but they were all getting minted in jobs half of them weren't even properly qualified for, so why rock the boat? The longer it took the better. When it came to the design of Horizon, let's just say misdiagnosing errors was common, and applying poorly written code to fix those errors was even more so. Don't get me wrong, there were some good, really hard working staff, but the managers, they were something else. The environment was toxic from the off. Hey, don't take my word for it – listen to what the recent online reviews have said about working for the company...

REVIEWERS 1, 2, 3 ENTER.

SQ 9 - MUSIC CUE – REVIEWERS JINGLE.

**REVIEWER 1** – Take this from a sucka that has worked almost 5 years in Fujitsu. Management are selected as part of an inner circle of friends and have no people or technical skills. Bad pay, bad IT systems, no sense of direction in a reactive not proactive work environment. You're also paid peanuts – peanuts without the nut and just the shell... Pros to working there - free drinks machine, and you could walk away any time you wanted because no one cared. Cons to working there – being there; the building existing.

**REVIEWER 2** – During my time at Fujitsu there was a lack of support and customers were abusive daily and we were given no training on how to handle them. I did not feel there was appropriate support for new staff. Pros to working there – it was my first IT job, I made some friends and learnt on the job. Cons – poor management, lack of appropriate support and a low salary.

**REVIEWER 3** – Great place to get your foot in the door with IT, but a terrible place to progress. The management were picked from a toy box and their skills were awful. Pros to working there - nope, can't think of any. Cons – bad management.

MUSIC JNGLE ENDS.

*FUJITSU BOSS ENTERS (40+ either gender) he sits, playing 'snake' on his old school Nokia mobile.*

**FUJITSU IT** - So after my first month at the place, my boss, who shall remain nameless, called me in for a meeting.

**FUJITSU BOSS** – Come in, come in. So you've been here a while, how are you finding your feet at Fujitsu?

**FUJITSU IT** – I'm finding my feet more easily than your team are finding the bugs in Horizon.

**FUJITSU BOSS** – Ah, well that's normal. There's always a few bugs in any new computer software...

**FUJITSU IT** – This isn't just a few bugs. The whole design is a nightmare! Half the team I'm working with don't really seem to care about solving the issues. Their morale is virtually non existent. They come in and write a bit of code and go home. Considering you're already spending ten million pound a month on this thing, I would have thought there would be more co-ordination of the design among the workforce?

**FUJITSU BOSS** – That's why we have you. I'm sure you'll soon whip them into shape!

**FUJITSU IT** – You're supposed to launch this thing in every Post Office across the country in six months time, right?

**FUJITSU BOSS** – Correct.

**FUJITSU IT** – I can't see how it's going to be ready on time. There's been over one hundred Category A bugs to fix since I got here. The whole thing needs throwing out and redesigning from scratch.

**FUJITSU BOSS** – Any substantial change this late would be impossible. I'm sure you'll find a way to make it work! (Looking at phone) Look at that! Highest ever score on snake!

*FUJITSU BOSS EXITS.*

**FUJITSU IT** – So they rolled Horizon out. Was it fit for purpose? Was it fuck.

*FUJITSU IT EXITS / POSTMASTER 1 & 3 ENTER.*

## 6) POSTMASTERS & MR PIGGERTON

**POSTMASTER 3** – 13 years we ran the branch, and it was a real success. There were holidays abroad for our family and plenty of presents around the tree at Christmas. Our kids were leaving the nest and soon there would be weddings and grandchildren to look forward to. It was 2009 when we had the first serious shortfall, and after that there wasn't a single week that year where I could get the books to balance. First it was £2000 down, and while I was desperately tried to find where it had gone, it jumped to £12,000 the next day. I couldn't understand it! So you started suspecting your staff, which was horrible, because these were honest, decent people who had worked for us for years, and hadn't taken a penny. I didn't want to worry our Gina about it all, so I made good on the losses from our savings, but by the time I'd covered shortfall number seven the branch had now swallowed £35,000 of our own money! All of our savings! I didn't know what to do, but I just hoped somehow, it would all still work out.

**POSTMASTER 1** – Then just like that we were £75,000 down! We'd had small shortfalls now and then but always covered them, out of our own pocket mind; but £75,000 was a huge amount of money! I called the help line, but on balance days it took forever to get through to them. So my district rep from the National Federation of Sub-Postmasters, Mr Piggerton, agreed to meet with me, at the local pub of course.

*MR PIGGERTON ENTERS – Wearing a shirt and tie, their breath laboured, carrying two menus. They sit opposite POSTMASTER 1.*

**MR PIGGERTON** – I think I'll have the sirloin Mrs Smith. I recall it was very good last time.

**POSTMASTER 1** – Yes, I recall you decided it was my shout last time.

**MR PIGGERTON** – Did I? Now look, £75,000 is a rather large sum of money to just simply disappear! Are you sure you haven't miscalculated somewhere?

**POSTMASTER 1** – I'm 100 percent sure! We've been through everything twice. I'm sure there's an issue with our Horizon terminal. Perhaps something is amiss with the main system back at Fujitsu? A duplication of figures somewhere, or something?

**MR PIGGERTON** – No, no, no, no no. I don't think so, my dear. I've complete confidence in the robustness of the Horizon system. It's literally managing hundreds of millions of transactions every week for 12,000 branches all over the UK. Besides it's developed by Fujitsu...

**POSTMASTER 1** – I'm not really sure what difference that makes Mr Piggerton?

**MR PIGGERTON** – Well the clue's in the name isn't it? I mean East Asia... Fujitsu. (whispering) The Japanese, computers are their thing, aren't they? It's right up at the top of their CV, it's what they're known for, well that and bombing Pearl Harbour...

**POSTMASTER 1** – And you're absolutely sure no one else at any other Post Office branch, anywhere in the country, has been reporting any problems similar to our own?

*MR PIGGERTON deliberately turns upstage, away from the audience. (hides behind the menu).*

**MR PIGGERTON** – No, no, no, no... nothing like this at all.

*Emerging from behind the menu MR PIGGERTON'S nose is now a pig nose.*

**POSTMASTER 1** – Your nose. Is it longer?

**MR PIGGERTON** – I don't know what you mean? Look, I really think you will have more success in solving this issue if you can find a different reason for your discrepancies.

**POSTMASTER 1** – A £75,000 shortfall appearing overnight is considerably more than a discrepancy, Mr Piggerton! Can't our union do something? You're supposed to represent me. You're supposed to represent all of us! What's the point of having a National Federation of Subpostmasters if it doesn't represent the Subpostmasters? He really made that Pearl Harbour joke by the way.

*NARRATOR ENTERS / POSTMASTER 1 EXITS (MR PIGGERTON remains in situ).*

### 7) THE NFSP BANQUET CONFERENCE

**NARRATOR** – What point indeed? Postal workers, your Postman Pats if you like, they had the Communication Workers Union, but the Subpostmasters had the NFSP, or 'the Fed', which was overseen by a committee of sorts. The Union General Secretary for most of the time we are concerned with, was a one George Thomson, a staunch defender of the Horizon system. The senior members of the NFSP, or National Federation of Subpostmasters, met up for their annual conference in a beautiful coastal hotel, their banner hanging above the committee table. I said their banner hanging from....

*SQ10 – SOUND FX – ATMOS -BANQUET SOUND FX.*

*The NARRATOR points towards the back wall waiting for the banner to unfurl, but it does not. FEDS 1, 2, 3, 5, ENTER, all dressed up, wearing pig noses and bibs. FED ONE carries a cigar and is almost Winston Churchill like in their demeanour. They carry glasses & bottles of Moet champagne. (Other members of the company may well play additional pigs, I mean Feds).*

**NARRATOR** – What happened to the banner?

*FED 4 points to the set and FED 1 (The Chairman) unfurls a tiny banner in the miniature set.*

**NARRATOR** – Anyway!!!! The Federation of Subpostmasters met for their annual conference...

*NARRATOR EXITS.*

*MR PIGGERTON is FED 4, but the same character.*

**FED 1** – Members of the Elected Executive Council of the National Federation of Subpostmasters, welcome one and all to what has been a very profitable year for the Post Office and our membership. I am pleased to announce as we soar through another profitable decade, that our union now has over 6,400 members...

*Everyone cheers!*

**FED 1** – This elected council of thirteen members proudly provides an umbrella of support and wisdom to its members over ten districts.

*FED 4 (MR PIGGERTON) begins to count the members of the council with their fingers, looking confused as to why there's only five of them. Everyone cheers!*

**FED 3** – Its regions, not districts.

**FED 1** – We proffer our wisdom and support over ten regions. Now nothing is more important to this Elected Council than its members, our good Subpostmasters, should always be seen as equals with our partner Post Office Ltd. Ask not what your union can do for you, but what your union can do for the Post Office!

**ALL FEDS** – (Everyone cheers loudly and grunts)

**FED 2** – Erm sorry, shouldn't that be the other way round?

**FED 1** – Now members of this Elected Executive Committee, a committee which has always been elected freely, and fairly without any unfair or undue influence... (pointing to the back of audience) Oh I see you there Johnny, thank you for sorting my Bentley, it's so nice to have it back in the drive. Broom! Broom! Now where was I? I call to order this special meeting to confirm our support for the new Post

Office Bill... could someone read out what was agreed while I finish my starter?

*FED 1 proceeds to eat loudly as FED 4 speaks, causing them to pause frequently.*

**FED 4** (standing) – This Federation supported the Government's Postal Service Bill at the All Party Post Office Group on Wednesday 24th November in the House of Commons - now that was a good piss up...

**ALL FEDS** – (rapping the table) Yes... yes indeed.

**FED 3** – Get on with it! We've another eight courses to get through yet!

**FED 4** – ...we announced at that meeting with immediate effect we are affiliating to the Employees Ownership Association, propelling us ever further toward turning Post Office Limited into a mutually owned company.

**ALL FEDS** – Hear! Hear!

**FED 1** – Very good. Before we do indeed indulge in our next course, I understand there is a most urgent matter requiring this committee's attention! Read it out would you, there's a good chap...

**FED 3** – It has come to our attention that a very urgent matter needs addressing by this council. And if this issue is not addressed immediately, it could undermine the very thing this council stands for. The heart of our members!

**ALL FEDS** – The heart of our members!

**FED 3** – So it is imperative, for the sake of our membership, for their reputations and this Federation's future that we must make a decision on this very important issue today!

**ALL FEDS** – Hear! Hear!

**FED 5** – Is this the issue with the Horizon system?

**FED 3** – No. There is no issue with Horizon. It's...

**ALL FEDS** – Completely robust!

**FED 2** – Sorry, so what is this crucially important issue we have to talk about then?

**FED 3** – I am of course talking about the most crucial issue of our Federation, ladies and gentleman. Approving the new design for the logo of the National Federation of Subpostmasters!

**ALL FEDS** – Oh yes! That's very important! etc etc.

**FED 5** – Well... Let's see it then!

*FED 3 gestures to the back wall for the logo...*

**FED 3** – The new logo... Ah... wait a minute...

*FED 3 moves to the miniature set and reveals the new logo. The logo is divided into four sections – a rose, a dragon, a harp and a thistle – However someone has painted a cock on it. The FEDS all jump to their feet and crowd around the miniature set, blocking it from the audience.*

**FED 3** – (pointing at the model) The new logo!!!

**FED 1** – It's a bit small. I was expecting a somewhat bigger mock up.

**FED 4** – I don't remember a flaccid cock being part of the discussion at the design meeting!

**FED 3** – What? That shouldn't be there. Anyway, erm, it's a work in progress.

*EVERYONE sits back down.*

**FED 1** – Right. Very good. All in favour of the new logo?

**FED 4** – Can we wait until we see it without the penis/genitalia on it?

**FED 2** – I don't know, I quite like it.

**FED 1** – Fine. All in favour of holding over the logo to the next meeting?

**ALL FEDS** (Raising hands) Aye.

**FED 1** – So carried.

**FED 2** – Mr Chairman, I really feel that I should mention before we close any other business that we've had 41 convictions of our members this year for false accounting. I'm only including convictions which were based on Horizon data.

**FED 1** – Ah, 41 is an excellent result then! Those auditors must be working hard, catching 41 thieves.

**FED 2** – Right... yes. We're all feeling confident there's no issues with Horizon then are we?

**FED 3** - If there really was an actual problem with the system, someone would have told us.

**FED 1** – Now look, just in case there's anything in it, I want complete assurances from Post Office that Horizon is working properly.

**FED 2** – (into a phone) Hello, is that the Post Office? Is Horizon working properly? Good. (puts phone down) They said it's definitely working. Very robust in fact.

**ALL FEDS** – VERY ROBUST!

*AUDIO CUE SOUND FX FADE.*

**FED 1** – Great, well I'm satisfied. What the next course?

**ALL FEDS** – OYSTERS!!!! (Parp!!!!)

*ALL FEDS RISE discussing the next course.*

*PM 5 ENTERS, chasing them off stage. FEDS EXIT.*

**POSTMASTER 5** – The Fed's website likes to re-write history, because clearly their challenges were useless. I'd been banging on their door for years, telling them there was something wrong with Horizon. They had no interest in even discussing it, and when I tried to hand out flyers warning other members at one of their earlier conferences, they spread rumours that I was crazy. To say they did absolutely nothing to help me would be the understatement of the year. Back then all their chairman cared about was finding ways to make more money.

POSTMASTER 5 EXITS.

SQ 11 MUSIC CUE – AUDITORS THEME.

AUDITORS 1 & 2 ENTER.

## 8) AUDITING PROMOTION TO SECURITY

*AUDITOR 1 is playing golf and carries a putter, lining up shots and moving the ball.*

**AUDITOR 1** – I have to say I do like the sound of more money sir....

**AUDITOR 2** – More money, exactly sir. And more money means a bigger villa in Marbella. You should apply too. The Security Team like applicants from the Auditing Department.

**AUDITOR 1** – What does this Internal Security Unit do then?

**AUDITOR 2** – It investigates internal security issues, obviously. Theft. And that can and will mean a person, or persons, flagged up by the Auditing Department. AKA, vis a vis by us.

**AUDITOR 1** – Ahhhhh... so mostly Subpostmasters and their staff then?

**AUDITOR 2** – Which is already our area of expertise sir.

**AUDITOR 1** – Indeed it is sir! But I'm not sure I want to quit the auditing department. I quite like the job satisfaction it brings me. Every day is different. I get to meet lots of different people, make them feel really uncomfortable, lock them out of their business premises. Make them squirm a bit. Ahhhhh, it makes you proud to be an Auditor.

**AUDITOR 2** – In the Internal Security Unit you'll get to do all of those things and more. You'll get to interrogate people under caution sir...

**AUDITOR 1** – You do know how much I like to interrogate people sir, but I'm not sure I want to give up on my auditor pay incentives.

**AUDITOR 2** – Would that be the incentive to our pay, determined by the number of branches we fail sir?

**AUDITOR 1** – It would indeed sir!

**AUDITOR 2** – You see, since Horizon has been installed in all the branches in our beloved green and pleasant land, I've noticed this little trend which I think will be to our benefit.

**AUDITOR 1** – What would that be then sir?

**AUDITOR 2** – Prior to Horizon coming in, very few Subpostmasters were actually convicted for theft. I mean their contract makes them liable for their own losses, so they'd essentially be stealing from themselves.

**AUDITOR 1** – Not much of an incentive to steal sir.

**AUDITOR 2** – Indeed not sir. But if you look here on the chart...

*AUDITOR 2 pulls down a tiny chart (hidden in the miniature set).*

**AUDITOR 1** – I'm not sure the audience can see that really tiny weeny chart sir.

**AUDITOR 2** – As I explained in the Anagram earlier...

**AUDITOR 1** – Metaphor...

**AUDITOR 2** – Right matador, that's what I said. Now if you look closely you'll see the Subpostmasters we've been prosecuting have been divided into several different categories according to their race...

**AUDITOR 1** - Their race sir? Let me see that. Siamese, dark skinned European types, there's even one beginning with the letter 'No' sir! I think some people might find this a bit racialist!

**AUDITOR 2** – We will let the public inquiry worry about that sir. So one year after Horizon comes in, in the year 2000 we have six criminal convictions of Sub-Postmasters and/or their employees using Horizon evidence.

**AUDITOR 1** – Nice. In 2001?

**AUDITOR 2** – 41 people convicted, using Horizon evidence.

**AUDITOR 1** – I like where there is going son, and in 2002?

**AUDITOR 2** – Sixty-four. By my calculations with Horizon providing us with so much evidence of criminal activity, we should be looking at a pretty big bonus pay cheque.

**AUDITOR 1** – We'd best not find any of them innocent then sir...

**AUDITOR 2** – Indeed not sir. Guilty of false accounting until proven innocent, as they say.

**AUDITOR 1** – I think I'll start looking for that villa with a nice pool in Marbella sir.

**AUDITOR 2** – I think I will too sir.

**AUDITOR 1** – So tell me more about this Internal Security Unit?

**AUDITOR 2** – You get to wear a long black coat, and act just like you're in the Matrix sir.

**AUDITOR 1** – Really? Fuck it! I'm in sir!

*AUDITORS EXIT / POSTMASTER 5 ENTERS.*

*SQ 12 MUSIC CUE – ATMOS TRACK.*

**9) SHORTFALLS**

**POSTMASTER 5** – As a Subpostmaster, when faced with a shortfall which you were ultimately responsible for, you had a couple of options. In the early days you could park shortfalls into something called a '*Suspense Account*', the idea being the situation would right itself in a day or two and all would be fine when you'd come to balance the books for your branch on Wednesday, so you wouldn't need to cover anything. The reality meant this was a way of parking a debt of money that you still owed to the Post Office. After they got rid of the suspense accounts, your second and only choice was to make good on the missing money immediately from your own pocket. When I had my first shortfall I absolutely refused to do either of these things. I knew my way around computers and was certain therein lay the problem. So in order to verify there was an issue with Horizon, I needed to get a look inside the thing, and interrogate the machine to find out exactly what had gone wrong. Unfortunately I was then informed there was literally no way to do this.

*POSTMASTERS 2 & 4 ENTER, 5 gives them a nod.*

**POSTMASTER 2** – First I was a few hundred pounds down, then one day it was two thousand, the next day it was six GRAND!!! I worked into the night trying to make sense of it all, but no matter what I did, I couldn't get Horizon to balance. I could see the locals peering through the window while I did everything I could to find the problem. I went to bed exhausted at 2 am, the issue still unresolved. Even then I couldn't sleep. I mean how was this still happening? I knew I hadn't taken the money and I ruled out everyone else who had any access to it. It could only be Horizon at fault but there was no way for me to prove it.

**POSTMASTER 4** – When my shortfall amount reached £20,000 I knew it was only a matter of time before they would call in the auditors! We're not supposed to have large sums of money on the premises you see, in case we get robbed. So when it reaches a certain amount, Post Office Ltd is automatically alerted. That part of their system worked remarkably well, funny that, eh? In the end I called my Area Manager. They came over but they were totally useless and simply told me to call the Horizon helpline.

*MANUAL ATMOS TRACK FADES OUT.*

*POSTMASTERS 3 & 1 ENTER.*

## 10) THE HELL LINE

*HELPLINE ONE, HELPLINE TWO, HELPLINE THREE ENTER (bringing chairs and phone / folder props as required). They sit in a line downstage close to the audience, dressed in casual attire, wearing headsets. They all have an air of indifferent about them.*

*The POSTMASTERS are stood upstage and slightly to the side of each HELPLINE operator.*

*AUDIO CUE – A phone rings. HELPLINE ONE answers.*

**HELPLINE 1** – Horizon helpline. What's your issue?

**POSTMASTER 4** – I'm having these HUGE discrepancies, so I need to access my Horizon terminal for the branch.

**POSTMASTER 5** - That way I can check the transactions on the computer system and make sure the system is not in error.

**HELPLINE 1** – The system can't be in error. Have you tried turning your terminal off and on again?

**POSTMASTER 3** – I told you last time, I've already tried that!

**POSTMASTER 4** - How is that going to balance my accounts?

**POSTMASTER 5** - I need to access my accounts on the Horizon system!

**HELPLINE 2** – I'm afraid I can't access your Horizon system from here.

**ALL POSTMASTERS** – WHAT? WHY NOT?

**POSTMASTER 3** – How are you supposed to check for faults if you can't access the system?

**HELPLINE 3** – Have you tried turning it off and on again?

**POSTMASTER 5** – Like I told you, I did that already!

**POSTMASTER 4** - Look this money has to be going somewhere!

**POSTMASTER 2** - It can't have just disappeared!

**HELPLINE 3** – Let me take you through these steps again.

**POSTMASTER 5** – As I've already explained to you, I have done all of those things already several times!

**HELPLINE 3** – Yes but in order to help you, I have to take you through the steps in my manual... so have you tried turning your Horizon terminal off and on again?

**POSTMASTER 5** – Jesus Christ give me strength!

**HELPLINE 1** – Has that corrected the issue?

**POSTMASTER 2** – No, it hasn't. This is the 200th time I've called you. Other people must be having these issues!

**HELPLINE 1** – You're the first person I've dealt with who's had an accounts issue with Horizon.

**POSTMASTER 3** – Look I've followed your instructions to clear this discrepancy...

**HELPLINE 1** – Very good and has that cleared your shortfall?

**POSTMASTER 3** – No... actually you've now doubled it for me. It's now £6000!!!

**POSTMASTER 4** – It's now £12,000!

**POSTMASTER 5** – Now its £30,000!

**POSTMASTER 2** - God, you're supposed to be fixing this!

**POSTMASTER 3** - You're supposed to be the help line and I am desperate for help!

**HELPLINE 2** – Ah, erm, that shouldn't have happened. Have you tried turning it off and on again?

*EVERYONE FREEZES – POSTMASTER 1 ENTERS.*

**POSTMASTER 1** – Every time I called them I was constantly treated as if I was the cause of the problem. It couldn't possibly be the fault of their damned Horizon system.

**HELPLINE 1** – Horizon is a flawless system.

**HELPLINE 2** - Its design is completely robust.

**HELPLINE 3** – It's impossible for Horizon to have made a mistake that would result in the kind of losses you describe. You must have done something wrong.

**POSTMASTER 3** – But other people must be having similar problems!

**HELPLINE 1** - No one else is having these kinds of problems.

**HELPLINE 2** – If the system was at fault, we'd be getting these kinds of calls all the time.

**HELPLINE OPERATORS** (All) – All the time.

**POSTMASTER 4** – And you're absolutely 100% sure no one else can access my terminal or my accounts at any time? Not someone at the Post Office, not an engineer from Fujitsu?

**HELPLINE 2** – There is absolutely no access to your terminal from an external source.

**HELPLINE 1** – Remote access to your account is completely impossible.

**POSTMASTER 3** – Now I've got a letter saying that I'm liable for this money! When I took over this Post Office I wasn't even shown a contract until six months later! Why was that?

**HELPLINE 2** – I'm sorry, but that really has really got nothing to do with us.

**POSTMASTER 4** – I called you to fix this problem. All you have managed to do is double my shortfall! Now I have to pay back twice as much!

**HELPLINE 3** – I'm sorry, but that really has got nothing to do with us.

**POSTMASTER 5** – You don't understand. I'm going to lose my shop...

**HELPLINE 1** – I'm sorry, that really has got nothing to do with us.

**POSTMASTER 1** – I can't leave the house without getting stared at! Everyone in the village thinks I stole the missing money!

**POSTMASTER 3** – Do you have any idea of the stress this is causing me and my family?

**POSTMASTER 4** – I'm not eating. I'm not sleeping!

**ALL POSTMASTERS** – I'm going to lose my business.

**HELPLINE OPERATORS** (All) – I'm sorry, this really has got nothing to do with us!

*POSTMASTERS 3, 4, 2 – EXIT / HELPLINES FREEZE.*

**POSTMASTER 1** – I don't know where their 'Hell Line' call centre was based, but they were completely useless and frequently made the situation worse. It was also blatantly obvious they didn't actually understand how Horizon worked. They must have had even less training on Horizon than we did.

**HELPLINE 1** – I had a day's training...

**HELPLINE 2** – I had four hours training, no wait, I had an hour for lunch so it would have been three hours.

**HELPLINE 3** – I can't remember how much training I actually had. I mean I wasn't even really listening. I've always been told I've got a great personality for customer service. I don't really focus on the technical things, I just answer the phone.

**POSTMASTER 1** – I wonder how many Horizon complaints the Hell Line logged from 1999 until the present day. I'd certainly like to know. (Looking at the Operators)

*SNAP TO BLACK / POSTMASTER 1 EXITS.*

*SQ 13 AUDIO CUE – Crackling flames.*

*SNAP TO RED WASH / The HELPLINE OPERATORS put on Devil horns.*

**HELPLINE OPERATORS** (All) – I'm sorry, but that really has got nothing to do with us... Yah ha ha hah!

*HELPLINE OPERATORS EXIT.*

## 11) IT'S ALL GOING PETE TONG (MONOLOGUES)

**POSTMASTER 5** - You have to understand it was the early 2000s when these issues first arose, so well before social media. No Facebook, no Instagram, no Twitter, no Tock Tick... So when I was told by the 'Hell Line' that I was the only person having this problem, I had no way of knowing if that were true. But I didn't leave it there. In addition to my leaflet campaign, I wrote to the Post Office head office several times. I stated unequivocally that it was unreasonable of the Post Office to hold me personally liable for these discrepancies until they could prove to me without a shadow of a doubt that Horizon was functioning exactly as it should be. The only response I received to this correspondence was a financial demand for the £2000!!! They were also quick to remind me that my contract made me legally liable for this mysterious missing sum. So, I started a website – Post Office Victims. I was certain there would be others in the same situation and I was going to find them.

*FUJITSU IT ENTERS / POSTMASTER 5 EXITS.*

**FUJITSU IT** – (to audience member) Loving those threads bruv, gotta get me some of those. You must be a lawyer for the Post Office with a suit like that. Don't forget to claim the ticket back on expenses, yeah? So look, when it comes to computer systems, especially one as complex as Horizon, the bigger the system, the harder they fall, you get me. I'm not sure why or who pushed the narrative that we'd created this infallible software. No software is infallible. I mean how many times do you get a five hour update for your XBOX, you get me? (whispering at the audience) My ID is NicebutDim007 if anyone wants to add me for a game of Call of Duty. With Horizon, errors were constantly happening. So we would create patches to fix these errors, only we couldn't create as many as we needed. Why? Budget cuts. Plus those working on the development side tended not to work in tandem with those of us fixing all the bugs. So you'd have them tossers in development still using any old bit of shit code, full of unresolved issues - which only added to the problem, you know what I mean bruv? There were all kinds of other errors too! I don't wanna get all technical on you, cause you know, you don't have Woodwork GSCE like me. Let me put it in terms you can understand. The Horizon system was as robust as the cladding on Grenfell tower was fireproof. In my opinion it was shite basically, and we were forever playing catch up.

*FUJITSU IT EXITS / POSTMASTERS 3 & 4 ENTER (3 has their hand in a bandage).*

*SQ14 MUSIC CUE – MONOLOGUES ATMOS TRACK.*

**POSTMASTER 3** – After the third massive shortfall at the branch my family noticed my constant change in mood. How could they not? The old me just wasn't there any more. I was withdrawn and moody all the time and my wife kept asking me 'Are you sure nothing's wrong?' - I mean who knew me better than her? Then just like that we had another shortfall of £23,000. I reported it straight away and we had to close the branch, and I was suspended until I made good on that money. Can you imagine what that's like? Someone cleaning out your bank account of everything you've grafted for all your life, who insists you stole from them, when you know it's not true? Imagine what that does to you...

**POSTMASTER 4** – Things could be hectic at our branch from time to time, but before those shortfalls it was nothing I couldn't deal with. I mean, I had three young children at home, so I could handle a full plate. When the weather was nice we'd have a barbecue in the garden and everyone would bring a dish and we'd all catch up on each other's gossip. I remember sitting there watching my children running around, playing with their friends, everyone enjoying my secret spicy chicken recipe, (whispering) crushed chilli sauce from Morrison's. I think that was the last time I was really happy. Once those shortfalls at our branch began, it was difficult to think about anything else. I'd just paid off that £24,000 by borrowing money from my parents, when we were suddenly out again by another £36,000. I didn't understand it. How could we be down by that much money? If I wasn't taking it, where was it all going?

*POSTMASTER 4 sits at the back of the stage, head bowed.*

**POSTMASTER 3** – I found it hard to hide my sense of shame, and I wore that label well, and I hadn't even earned it. I still went to the cricket club on the odd Sunday, but I didn't play any more. I let someone else take my spot on the team and I'd sit back and I'd find a quiet spot and become part of the furniture. I'd watch the game but my mind would glaze over because all I could think about was the missing money and how all our bank accounts were empty, every credit card maxed out to the hilt. There were no more holidays, not even our favourite spot in the Lake District. We had four presents under the tree that year. Four. By the end of 2013, another £57,000 had gone missing over twenty two months. I ended up borrowing from everyone I could to cover it. My parents sold their car and gave me all their savings. It was like a never-ending black hole - then to top it all we were robbed.

AUDITOR 1 ENTERS (Long coat) – picks up a chair which POSTMASTER 3 sits on.

ATMOS TRACK FADES OUT HERE.

**POSTMASTER 3** - I was just doing the parcel handover to the Postman when they burst in, jamming the door with a crowbar, slamming it down on my hand. (slams down chair) They got behind the till, stole another £54,000. You'd think they would have offered me counselling after that experience. Nope...

## 13) OH WHAT A LOVELY DAY FOR INTERROGATION

AUDITOR 2 ENTERS (Dressed as Security Team). AUDITOR 1 sets out the other chairs as they speak.

**AUDITOR 1** – This will go so much easier for you if you just admit you were in on the robbery at the branch, right sir?

**AUDITOR 2** – Absolutely sir.

**POSTMASTER 3** – I keep telling you, I didn't have anything to do with the robbery! For Christ's sake, look at the state of my hand.

**AUDITOR 1** – Are you sure you didn't do that to yourself sir?

**POSTMASTER 3** – I've got three broken fingers and a shattered wrist!

**AUDITOR 1** – You could have deliberately shut that in the car door sir!

**POSTMASTER 3** – If I was going to stage a robbery, I can think of less painful ways to do it.

**AUDITOR 1** – You see the problem is, this isn't the first time money has gone missing from your branch is it Mister....

**AUDITOR 2** – (Whispering) Mr Smith... We're not using real names for the actual Subpostmasters as they're anagrams of more than one person...

**AUDITOR 1** – Amalgamations sir, they're amalgamations of several real people.

**AUDITOR 2** – Right - Amalgagram, that's what I said.

**AUDITOR 1** – Right, Mister, erm... Smith. You've got quite the long list of financial discrepancies over the years at your branch haven't you....

**POSTMASTER 3** – Only since we started using bloody Horizon!

**AUDITOR 2** – Totalling over one hundred thousand pounds...

**POSTMASTER 3** – Yeah, and don't I know it! I paid for every single one of them out of my own pocket!

**AUDITOR 2** – You did admit that the security door was open at the time of the robbery?

**POSTMASTER 3** – Of course it was open! I was handing over the parcels for collection at the time! It's normal procedure! I have to open the door!

**AUDITOR 1** – Normal procedure he says, during a robbery?

**POSTMASTER 3** – I didn't know there was going to be a robbery until it happened!

**AUDITOR 2** – I don't think it's looking very good for you Mr Smith, is it sir?

**AUDITOR 1** – Indeed not sir. It never pays to be a thief.

**BOTH AUDITORS** – WHERE'S THE MONEY?

**POSTMASTER 3** – I've already told you, God knows how many times! These other shortfalls have to have been caused by a fault in Horizon. Why would I steal money that I was legally liable for in the first place? Especially when I kept paying it back straight away anyway! It doesn't make any sense!

AUDITOR 2 – All men succumb to temptations when they're put in front of them.

AUDITOR 1 – Or women. Let's not leave them out sir.

AUDITOR 2 – Men, women and all genders in-between are capable of succumbing to the temptations of sin!

POSTMASTER 3 – I've never stolen anything in my life! There's got to be something wrong with Horizon! Why don't you investigate Fujitsu who made the damn thing? Maybe someone there is stealing the money? I can't have been the only branch having problems like this?

POSTMASTER 3 FREEZES / POSTMASTERS 1, 2, 4 & 5 ENTER, sitting on different seats.

AUDITOR 1 – I'm afraid you are Mr Smith.

AUDITOR 2 – The only one with any trouble at all.

AUDITOR 1 – (To Postmaster 2) Just after the money went missing from your branch, you and several members of your family took a rather expensive holiday to the Dominican Republic.

POSTMASTER 2 – It was my parents wedding anniversary! They paid for me to go out of their own pocket! I didn't take any money!

AUDITOR 2 – Maybe you wanted some extra money for cocktails and souvenirs?

AUDITOR 1 – If you purchased expensive gifts, you know we're going to find them.

POSTMASTER 2 – I brought back a fridge magnet and you're welcome to it.

AUDITOR 1 – How much did this diamond encrusted fridge magnet cost exactly?

POSTMASTER 2 – I think it was 20,000 pesos.

**BOTH AUDITORS** – Aha! Twenty thousand pounds!

**POSTMASTER 2** – I said 20,000 pesos. Actually now I think about it, it was 2000 pesos.

*AUDITORS move on to POSTMASTER 1.*

**AUDITOR 1** – You should just come clean Mrs...

**AUDITOR 2** – Smith.

**AUDITOR 1** – Mrs Smith. As your lawyer has advised you, if you plead guilty to false accounting you'll likely get a shorter prison sentence.

**POSTMASTER 1** – Prison? But I haven't stolen anything!

**AUDITOR 2** – That £74,000 just sprouted legs and ran off on its own then did it?

**POSTMASTER 1** – Check my accounts, check our property, you won't find anything!

*AUDITORS move on to POSTMASTER 4.*

**AUDITOR 1** – You might as well just admit the theft and tell us where the money is. The proceeds of crime act allows us to come after your property...

**AUDITOR 2** – Indeed we can come after all your worldly goods.

**POSTMASTER 4** – I'm not admitting to a crime that I haven't committed!

**AUDITOR 1** – Well someone took £22,000 from your Post Office and I don't think it was the tooth fairy. It wasn't the tooth fairy was it sir?

**AUDITOR 2** – It wasn't the tooth fairy sir, nor do I think it was the Easter Bunny.

**POSTMASTER 4** – The Easter Bunny leaves you chocolate, they don't steal things...

**AUDITOR 1** – Exactly Mrs Smith. If you've been having all these problems for so long, why didn't you call the helpline to get them resolved?

**POSTMASTER 4** – I did call the helpline! Thirty-nine times. They were fucking useless!

**AUDITOR 1** – Getting upset isn't going to help you Mrs Smith!

**AUDITOR 2** – No. Definitely not going to help sir.

**POSTMASTER 5** – Upset? Of course I'm upset! I'm completely innocent and you're treating me like a criminal.

*AUDITORS move back to POSTMASTER 2.*

**AUDITOR 1** – Of course if you just plead guilty to false accounting...

**AUDITOR 2** – Then you'll get a lesser sentence.

**AUDITORS BOTH** – Just admit to taking the money.

**ALL POSTMASTERS** – I didn't take the money!

**AUDITORS BOTH** – Plead guilty to false accounting!

*The AUDITORS move accordingly. Back to POSTMASTER 1.*

**POSTMASTER 1** – God! I can't go to prison!

**AUDITORS BOTH** – Just plead guilty!

**POSTMASTER 1** – I can't! I'm pregnant!

*SNAP TO BLACK / AUDITORS, POSTMASTERS 3, 4 & 5 EXIT.*

**14) NO LONGER ALONE**

*SQ 15 MUSIC CUE – MONOLOGUES ATMOS TRACK - (LX SPECIAL POSTMASTER 1).*

*POSTMASTER 1 stands.*

**POSTMASTER 1** – It was right before my court case case when I discovered I was carrying my child. Thanks to my face being plastered all over the papers, the locals had stopped talking to us, no more quiz nights for us down the pub. When I went to the doctors the staff at the surgery gave me gave me bitchy vibes, looking over at me, pointing. Even my GP seemed to know all about my case. When my Doctor suggested I might want a termination in case I went to prison, I can't believe I nearly agreed to it. In my culture the life of a child is sacred. But then I thought, if I make that decision, if I take away the child's chance of having a life, my child... that's not me making that choice, that's the Post Office making it for me. So I thought - I'm having this baby no matter what happens. Those bastards already took our business, took our savings, they even took our house, but they were not having my child! No. Excuse my language, but I told my husband - 'Fuck the Post Office'. If I go to prison then I go to prison, but I am keeping this baby. 'That's the one thing they can't take away from us!' I told him. It was the first time I had seen him smile in a very long time. We cried a lot that night. Then... just before I went to court I got this phone call... who could have thought that a total stranger was going to be my best friend for life.

**POSTMASTER 2** – Everyone in my town knew about my court case. I mean, I'd lived there all my life so when the local paper decided to run a story with my picture slapped across the front page, how could they not. I might as well have been walking around with a 'wanted criminal' neon sign on my head. Fortunately, many of the locals took a different view and rallied round; some were even character witnesses when we got to court. But sadly it didn't make any difference. Because I wouldn't admit to theft, I got a year and did nine months. Some people never looked at me the same way. You know the saying goes 'No smoke without fire...' When I asked my mother how I was going cope, the last thing she said to me, just before I got convicted. 'You're so damn tough, you'll get through this, you will....' She died while I was inside. If you lost a relative during the pandemic but couldn't be with them at the end, then you'll know what this feels like. By the time others started doing their own investigations into the Post Office and Horizon, I'd already been in and out of prison, having served my time for this fictional crime. The St Johns Ambulance, who I'd volunteered with for years, told me my services were 'no longer required'. That hurt. I was one of the first to be convicted using Horizon evidence, so by the time I was released, for so many others this ordeal was just getting started. Somehow I got through the indignity of my time prison. This... (pointing to herself) this is just a front. It's how I get through the day. Inside, behind this mask, I'm totally broken. I just don't want them to see that, I won't give them that satisfaction. Then nearly a decade later, I read about this lady, same circumstances, now branded a thief, about to be tried for False Accounting, and somehow I managed to get her phone number...

ATMOS TRACK ENDS.

*On their phones, POSTMASTERS 1 & 2 stand at opposite ends of the stage.*

**POSTMASTER 1** – It's so nice to finally be speaking to someone who understands what I've been through!

**POSTMASTER 2** – I'm not the only one. Dozens have joined the cause, we just had our first meeting.

**POSTMASTER 1** – I heard, the Justice for Subpostmasters Alliance?

**POSTMASTER 2** – I know, it sounds like something from Star Wars doesn't it? People are finally starting to listen to us. Did you see the article written by Rebecca Thompson that I sent you in Computer Weekly?

**POSTMASTER 1** – Yes I saw it. I knew something was wrong with Horizon. Why won't the Post Office do something about it?

**POSTMASTER 2** – Because they can't afford to admit they've been wrong all along. Imagine the scandal it would cause.

**POSTMASTER 1** – Fat lot of good that's going to do me. The jury are going to send me to prison.. I just know it.

**POSTMASTER 2** – Listen, I know it's hard, believe me I know. I was in the same place once, but I got through it and you will too.

**POSTMASTER 1** – I don't know if I can...

**POSTMASTER 2** – You can and you will. Believe me. I didn't know how strong I really was until I had to do my sentence.

**POSTMASTER 1** – How did you cope?

**POSTMASTER 2** – Because I knew I was innocent and I believed the truth would come out one day, and we're going to make sure that happens. Look, worst case scenario - if you get a conviction then as soon as you get out you're going to join the fight alongside us. So you need hang on for that day, Okay?

**POSTMASTER 1** – Okay, I will... and thank you.

**POSTMASTER 2** – Just remember you're not alone in this fight any more.

*POSTMASTER 2 EXITS, POSTMASTER 3 ENTERS.*

**POSTMASTER 1** – (To audience) Then I got the call, the jury were back in. Guilty. I was going to prison...

*POSTMASTER 1 EXITS.*

### 15) TIP OF THE ICEBERG (MONOLOGUES)

**POSTMASTER 3** – Two months after the robbery I was sacked by the Post Office, and even though we had given them tens of thousands of pounds to cover their 'missing money', they still found that I was partially responsible for the robbery, so they sent me a further demand for £7,500. No one actually wanted to help me. As far as they were all concerned I might as well have been a criminal. I'd never felt so helpless in all my life. I became withdrawn and detached from everything and everyone around me. My wife, she tried... she really did. I just couldn't take it any more. Everyone has a breaking point and I'd reached mine.

*POSTMASTER 3 SITS (REMAINS ON) / POSTMASTERS 4 & 5 ENTER.*

**POSTMASTER 4** – After I was questioned by the Auditors I was cautioned and they 'suggested' we should go down to the local Police Station. I didn't even think to say no, or ask about a lawyer and even in the car they were still relentless, they kept telling me to admit I'd stolen the money and that I needed to pay it back. They even offered to take me to the bank to get the cash. I told them I didn't have that kind of money! I just kept saying 'No, no, I haven't stolen anything!' I asked to see evidence of this £50,000 shortfall. All they produced were the account reports that I signed and sent off to Chesterfield every week, telling me this was proof of false accounting. I told them 'If I'm a thief, I must be a lousy thief to be stealing from myself when I've already had to borrow money from my mother to pay you back.' When they said I was going to go to prison for a very long time, all I could think about was my three young children growing up without their mother. That was when I knew I had to get a lawyer – I couldn't let them do this to me! I asked them there and then if any other branches were having the same kind of issues - 'no, just you', they told me.

*POSTMASTER 4 EXITS.*

*SQ 16 MUSIC CUE – POSTMASTER 5 RAMBO TRACK.*

*POSTMASTER 5 slowly puts on a red bandana and combat jacket.*

**POSTMASTER 5** – The Post Office underestimated me. Between paying off the outgoing Postmaster and refurbishing the shop next door, my wife and I had spent over £100,000 of our savings on this business, and for what? To just let the Post Office come and in and take it all, just like that and leave us with nothing. There was no way I was going to let them get away with that. Excuse my French but they fucked with the wrong Postmaster that day. After that, as far as I was concerned this was war. I suspected what had happened to me was just the tip of the iceberg and that there must be others going through the same thing. I knew something was rotten with Horizon and I was going to find out what. Soon the Post Office Victims website I'd set up had a trickle of contacts, but after the 2009 article in Computer Weekly, soon there were more. Later that year The Justice for Subpostmasters Alliance was born. Soon there were thirty of us, then forty, then fifty and the number just kept going up. We got organised and ready for battle! If the Post Office wanted a fight, we were going to give them one!

*SQ 17 AUDIO CUE: The Rambo music comes to an abrupt halt, like an old vinyl record jumping the needle.*

**MRS BATES** – (off stage) Alan! Your dinners ready!

**POSTMASTER 5** – Yes dear, I'll be along in a moment.

**MRS BATES** – (off stage) It's getting cold, and no wearing the bandana at the dinner table please!

**POSTMASTER 5** – No dear.

*POSTMASTER 5 EXITS, removing their bandana as they depart.*

*POSTMASTER 3 ENTERS.*

*SQ 18 MUSIC CUE.*

**POSTMASTER 3** – It was my birthday earlier that week and my kids popped in and gave me a card and a present. 'Cheer up Dad, it will be okay, you'll see.' - 'I know...' I said, 'give us a hug...' That was the last time I saw them. The following Monday, the 23rd of September it was, I got up early as usual. Even though I'd been sacked, I was supposed to run the Post Office until the temporary branch manager arrived. I drove my usual route on the A41 and stopped in this little lay-by. I got out of the car and stood by the road. I thought about so many things in that moment – our decision to take on the Post Office as a business, how it had become this black hole that had swallowed every single penny I had. The way they'd treated me after the robbery, the total humiliation of it all. I thought about my family, my beautiful wife, my two children, and how lucky I'd been to have them all around me for so long. I couldn't escape this awful feeling that somehow this was all my fault and that I'd brought them this terrible shame. It was that shame I couldn't live with anymore. It had been a good life... until those people destroyed it all and took it from me. It's funny you know, I thought at least this is one decision I had control over, but I was lying to myself really. You see those people at the Post Office, they made it for me. I know I will cause everyone so much pain and I'm so sorry to you all that I had to leave. I saw the bus coming up the road, it was time to go. When your own pain is so, so great, you don't think about the consequences, you just want it to go away, you just want it to stop. So... I made it stop.

*AUDIO MANUAL – SHARP OFF (note the music here ends before the monologue ending).*

*SQ 19 - MUSIC MONOLOGUE ATMOS TRACK / NARRATOR ENTERS.*

**NARRATOR** - Four Subpostmasters that we know of, took their lives as a direct result of being persecuted by the Post Office. There would be more. It's easy to say the words 'Post Office' and think of it as this anonymous, faceless entity that acted with impunity. But the Post Office is run by actual people. You see, this story has many heroes, but damn, it has some real villains too. I mean talk about real criminals. When we come back, I think it's about time you met some of them.

*FADE TO BLACK / NARRATOR EXITS.*

*HOUSE / INTERVAL LIGHTS CUE.*

*SQ 20 - MUSIC CUE - INTERVAL MUSIC (15 minute track which takes out into the second half).*

*AUDITORS RE SET THE SCENE.*

**INTERVAL**

# 2

# ACT II - FALSE ACCOUNTS

*The six chairs have been set with three either side of the desk in a V formation, allowing for the best sight lines possible.*

**15) THE REBELLION BEGINS**

*SQ 21 - MUSIC CUE – MONOLOGUES ATMOS TRACK.*

*NARRATOR & POSTMASTER 1 ENTER.*

**NARRATOR** – While the Horizon disaster was unfolding, it first came to the attention of Post Office CEO Adam Crozier, who did absolutely nothing about it during his tenure, before moving on to another highly paid job elsewhere. Next was Paula Vennells. Promoted from within from her role as Group Network Director, by the time Vennells became CEO of the Post Office in 2012 there had already been over 600 prosecutions of Subpostmasters using Horizon evidence. Her appointment came with a generous salary and the objective of making the Post Office profitable by 2020. She was given a £1.34 billion pound government grant to help achieve this. It's hard to see where that money went, because under her tenure a few branches were given a new lick of paint while they closed down dozens more. They also cancelled most of the Subpostmaster salaries and left the ageing Horizon machines exactly where they were. By now several articles challenging the integrity of Horizon had appeared in Computer Weekly and Private Eye, but the press and media at large remained strangely silent. However, the ranks of Justice For Subpostmasters Alliance were growing. With the rise of social media, word was finally getting out that a small band of rebels were finally going to stand against the EMPIRE! (pause) of the Post Office.

**POSTMASTER 1** – On the final day of my court case, standing there in the dock, I was terrified. The prosecution stated in their summary that any problems with Horizon would surely be obvious for a Subpostmaster to spot. Really? We were never taught how to spot problems, so how would I know how to do that? I didn't build the bloody thing! My lawyer fought a good fight, but the Post Office wouldn't provide the transaction logs from Horizon, because they said 'It was too expensive to do so...' So it was up to us to prove Horizon wasn't working. Beyond the Horizon data, there was no other evidence of theft offered in my case, because they couldn't find any. The Judge still sentenced me to 15 months. As they led me out of the court I saw the smug faces of the Post Office legal team already celebrating. My conviction gave them further proof that Horizon was blameless. I exchanged one last glance with my distraught husband, sharing a look that we'd only give one another in our darkest moments. We knew our love for each other was all we had to keep us going. The Post Office had taken everything from us but I knew for the sake of my unborn child I had to survive this.

*NARRATOR & POSTMASTER 1 EXIT (manual music fade here) POSTMASTER 5 ENTERS – They're dressed in brown Jedi Robes.*

**POSTMASTER 5** – Postmaster 5 here, that's Mister, erm Smith to you. Forgive my attire - children's birthday party. Having marshalled the troops, our first meeting took place in November of 2009, in the small village hall of Fanny Backwater in darkest Warwickshire. We were a sorry sight to be sure, but saw in one another kindred spirits who had trodden the same unfortunate path. A motley crew of unjustly accused, who'd had our lives turned upside down by dark and evil forces that were difficult to comprehend. When our fellow rebels first gathered, over 500 Subpostmasters had been convicted of either theft or false accounting, 70 in 2009 alone. Going into 2013 that figure had reached 680. Of course we didn't know that back then, but by this time our growing membership were soon joined by sympathetic legal experts, like Kay Linnel. We were still a mouse going up against a lion, but I've heard that lions get easily scared of rodents.

*POSTMASTER 2 ENTERS, shivering, rubbing their hands (also dressed in Jedi Robes).*

**POSTMASTER 2** – Working central heating would be nice Mr Smith.

**POSTMASTER 5** – I'm not sure central heating has reached Fanny Backwater yet.

**POSTMASTER 2** – Oh and Julian called, he's going to be late today. I'll do the minutes until he gets here.

*POSTMASTER 4B – ENTERS, also wearing Jedi robes. 5 & 4B exchange a look. (Note in this scene PM4 is not playing the same character as in their monologues, hence 4B).*

**POSTMASTER 5** – That would be great thank you. Children's party?

**POSTMASTER 4B** – Halloween. God it's colder than a witches tit in here! Is there any tea and biscuits?

**POSTMASTER 2** – Yes, I've just put the kettle on.

**POSTMASTER 4B** - Good, no need to use the force then.

*POSTMASTER 1 ENTERS, also dressed in Jedi Robes, fishing through their bag, placing a Baby Yoda on the table. They also carry a newspaper.*

POSTMASTER 1 – Hello everyone... is this the Rebel, erm, Subpostmasters Alliance?

POSTMASTER 2 – Hey! You found us! Welcome!

*POSTMASTER 2 hugs POSTMASTER 1.*

POSTMASTER 1 - sorry about my attire, only I came straight from a...

POSTMASTERS - 4B, 5, 2 – ...A children's party?

POSTMASTER 1 – Yes, how did you know? (looking around and ...at the audience) Oh... Good turn out I see!

POSTMASTER 4B (looking at the audience) It's nice to see so many new faces here today.

POSTMASTER 2 – Shall we get started then? Item one on the agenda – Our good MP James Arbuthnot met with Post Office Chairman, or should that be chairwoman? Alice Perkins...

POSTMASTER 4B – She's married to Jack Straw by the way...

POSTMASTER 2 – Yes handy to have friends in high places. He said Perkins and the Post Office Company Secretary Alwen Lyons were responsive to his concerns and promised the new Chief Executive Officer, a one 'Paula Vennells', would investigate the matter further.

POSTMASTER 1 – (producing a newspaper) Vennells, She's an Anglican priest, I just read her interview in The Daily Telegraph.

POSTMASTER 4B – Read out the highlights then...

POSTMASTER 1 – (reading) 'I saw the Post Office as something bigger and deeper..'.

POSTMASTER 4B – She sounds sexually frustrated to me... sorry, go on.

POSTMASTER 1 (continues) 'If you work for the Post Office you can't just focus on the commercial side by itself, it's about the community too. People care desperately for the Post Office.'

POSTMASTER 5 – I read that she told a business conference that she took: 'biblical inspiration from the young King Solomon, who showed humility in asking God for a wise and understanding heart, so that he could rule his people with justice...'

POSTMASTER 1 – A wise and understanding heart, with some actual justice thrown in, is certainly what we all need. Maybe she'll be sympathetic?

POSTMASTER 4B – Sounds like a self important cunt to me. (Everyone is shocked) What? I call them like I see them.

POSTMASTER 5 – Time will tell. Next item on the agenda?

POSTMASTER 2 – So, finally Post Office General Legal Counsel Susan Crichton has appointed forensic accountants, Second Sight, to independently investigate Horizon. They're a forensic accounting firm run by Ron Warmington and Ian Henderson.

POSTMASTER 4B – How did they get the job?

POSTMASTER 1 – I heard they were the cheapest. Apparently the new CEO loves to save money.

POSTMASTER 2 – Yes, but the one MP actually fighting our corner, James Arbuthnot, has approved them. They're looking at 13 of the first convictions that came about as a result of Horizon evidence. Including mine I believe.

POSTMASTER 1 – How do we know they'll be impartial?

POSTMASTER 5 – We don't, which is why we're going meet them ourselves, so I can look them in the eye. We've also secured a meeting with the new CEO herself. So I guess we'll get to see just how much of a 'See you next Tuesday' Ms Vennells is for ourselves, won't we?

*SQ22 - MUSIC CUE – End of Drunk3Po Rebellion / Return of Jedi style – (bleeds over into next scene fades out).*

POSTMASTER 2 *transforms into* ALICE PERKINS *on stage. (the audience is in on the joke) She chucks Baby Yoda off stage, replacing him with an Empire-like ornament.*

## 16) PROJECT SPARROW

POST OFFICE BOARD ENTER - ALWEN LYONS, BELINDA CROWE, SUSAN CRICHTON, ALICE PERKINS, *they sit. The board are all notably dressed in black apart from Critchton (Empire Officers uniforms as close as possible).*

**PERKINS** – I call to order this first meeting of the new Secret Sub-Committee for Project X. Alwen take notes please.

**LYONS** – Of course, and here's those recipes for those cakes you wanted...

**PERKINS** – Lovely. Right, to business then. We've already got Mark Davies & Alasdair Marnoch online, so present. Let's do the rest of the roll call.

**CRICHTON** – Shouldn't we wait until everyone else is here?

**PERKINS** – Susan Crichton, legal counsel for the Post Office.

**CRICHTON** – Present.

**PERKINS** – Angela Van Den Bogerd.

**BOGERD** – (off stage) Present!

**CROWE** - What does she do again?

ANGELA VAN DEN BOGERD, *a puppet, arrives from behind the curtain, hovering near* VENNELLS.

**BOGERD** – I'm the Network Operations Manager, brilliant and always completely transparent. Do we have time for me to waffle on for 90 minutes about how brilliant I am at everything?

### False Accounts - Exposing The Post Office Cover-Up

**PERKINS** – No, you did that last week. Bogerd, present. Alice Perkins, Company Secretary, oh that's me isn't it? (laughs) Present. Belinda Crowe, Programme Director of Project X...

**CROWE** – Present, and on that subject I really think we should change the name of our Secret Sub-Committee. I mean Project X... It automatically conjures up images of all sorts of dubious and illegal activities, which is exactly what I would have thought we want to avoid...

**PERKINS** – I'll add that topic to any other business, now we're just waiting for our CEO...

*SQ 23 - MUSIC CUE - EMPIRE MARCH (sharp manual fade out).*

*PAULA VENNELLS, (followed by JOHN SCOTT) ENTERS, she wears a black cloak and scowls around the room, everyone stands and bows. SCOTT carries the 'evidence bucket' and some documents.*

**VENNELLS** – You may sit.

*SCOTT looks for a chair, but is unable to find one. He stands off to one side.*

**PERKINS** – Don't worry about being late Paula, we were just getting started.

**VENNELLS** – You will address me as Lady Vennells, and a CEO is never late Ms Perkins, she arrives exactly when she means to. Now, I have good news to report. After extensive cost-cutting, we are back on target for 'Objective 2020'!

*Everyone looks confused.*

**BOGERD** – The Government's target deadline to make the Post Office operationally profitable!

**EVERYONE** (Improvised) - Oh yes, very good / of course / I'm brilliant etc etc.

**VENNELLS** – Good, then let us turn to more important matters. I welcome you all to the first of our secret committee meetings.

**CROWE** – Perhaps my Lord, I mean Lady Vennells, as I am the programme director of this secret committee, it might be helpful if I knew what its function was exactly? (Vennells glares) Or not Lady Vennells, whatever you think is best.

**VENNELLS** - This top secret committee has been put together because POL, and those who look to us to guide it, are concerned that the interim report from Forensic Accountants Second Sight, appears to be throwing some considerable doubt on the reliability of Horizon. Which as we all know is...

**EVERYONE** – Very robust!

**CROWE** – Sorry, I thought we were expecting Second Sight to completely exonerate us?

*The scene freezes. IAN HENDERSON ENTERS (male, 50+, suit, tie).*

**HENDERSON** – Ian Henderson of Second Sight here. Ian to my friends, forensic God to everyone else. Susan Crichton got us the job to investigate the Horizon issue on behalf of the Post Office. I liked Susan, she was straight forward and a decent sort, an exception to the rule among this group. When we first sat down with Alice Perkins and Paula Vennells, myself and my partner Ron, we were very clear in our remit.

*The scene unfreezes – HENDERSON is at the far end of the board. VENNELLS, PERKINS & BOGERD (Who sit together) look over at him.*

*SCOTT starts ripping up files/documents, placing them in a large bin in extravagant comical fashion.*

**HENDERSON** – If Second Sight are going to investigate on behalf of the Post Office, I want it to be absolutely clear that we are only interested in getting to the truth, not delivering you some kind of whitewash.

**VENNELLS** – But that is exactly what we all want Ian, can I call you Ian?

# False Accounts - Exposing The Post Office Cover-Up

**HENDERSON** – Mr Henderson.

**PERKINS** – Mr Henderson, Paula and I are only interested in getting to the bottom of the matter.

**VENNELLS** – Absolutely - your reputation precedes you, that is why you and Mr Warmington are here.

**HENDERSON** – You do understand, if our findings go against you, this could seriously damage your brand and undermine your business model?

**VENNELLS** – Mr Henderson, we are only interested in the truth and have every confidence you will find that this whole thing is nothing more than a few bad apples.

**HENDERSON** – Right, well Ron and I will get down to work then. Sorry can I just ask what that man is doing? (pointing to Scott)

*SCOTT freezes with a smile, hiding ripped documents behind his body.*

**VENNELLS** – Oh nothing, he's just storing some important files in our special evidence hole bin. I mean our secure storage area.

**HENDERSON** – Right. As long as he's not destroying any files we need to look at. (joking)

*EVERYONE LAUGHS – then with the raise of VENNELLS hand, abrupt silence.*

**PERKINS** – Our head of Network Operations, Angela Van Den Bogerd, will assist Second Sight with whatever you need.

*Waved away by VENNELLS, JOHN SCOTT EXITS.*

**BOGERD** – I'm absolutely brilliant at everything, and will be helpful and completely transparent at all times.

**HENDERSON** – Excellent. I would expect nothing less of our country's most trusted brand. So we will start with these thirteen cases and work forwards from there. We will require all files, emails, everything. I'm sure you know the Justice for Subpostmasters Alliance would like us to look at more.

**PERKINS** – We shall be sending a letter out to every branch in the country, informing them of your investigation and asking them to raise any concerns they might have of their own.

*PERKINS hands a copy of the letter to HENDERSON.*

**HENDERSON** – I see. Very good.

*EVERYONE FREEZES - HENDERSON stands, takes centre stage, addressing the audience.*

**HENDERSON** – So, buried rather deep in that letter was some very important wording. It stated:

**PERKINS** – 'Second Sight will be entitled to request information related to any concern from Post Office Limited and if we hold that information, Post Office Limited will provide it to Second Sight.'

**HENDERSON** – So with that in mind, I thought it was about time I went and visited Fujitsu.

*HENDERSON EXITS. The Sparrow Committee meeting comes back to life.*

## 17) KEEP CALM & CALL COUNSEL

**CRICHTON** – As your legal counsel, it is my duty to point out to this committee that our own barrister noted there was evidence reporting bugs in the Horizon system, which was not disclosed to the defence in previous cases. We summarised all this in a report. I think we really need to get behind the mediation scheme in good faith and try and get it to work.

*DEAD SILENCE – Everyone looks away. VENNELLS glares.*

**CRICHTON** - I am deeply concerned about all this, not least because I read correspondence in an email chain which suggests our head of security issued an order to delete all emails and destroy documents pertaining to both this legal advice and all matters voicing concerns on Horizon's reliability.

**CROWE** – Who is our head of security again?

**EVERYONE ELSE** – John Scott!

**VENNELLS** – Sound like he should get a bonus, make a note of it Perkins.

**PERKINS** – So noted Lord Vader... I mean Lady Vennells.

**CRICHTON** – Right. Firstly, we should not be destroying any evidence, and I think some of these convictions with Horizon evidence might not be legally robust...

*Everyone draws a huge breath, looking away from CRICHTON*

*SQ 24 - AUDIO SOUND FX CUE – BEATING HEART (Stops when Crichton dies below).*

**CRICHTON** – I really think it might be time to re-consider (choking) our position, as we could just... be... looking... at... the tip of the... iceberg....

**VENNELLS** – I find your lack of faith in our most trusted brand, and Horizon, disturbing. *VENNELLS stretches her hand out in a strangulation gesture.*

**CRICHTON** – I think we.... should really... start... a sincere mediation process... errrrrrr.

*CRICHTON slumps over dead. VENNELLS removes her dark gloves, thrusting them at BOGERD.*

**VENNELLS** - Angela, get rid of that mess would you...

*She points to the body which the BOGERD puppet attempts in vain to remove, resulting in CRICHTON'S head being banged on the table several times.*

**EVERYONE** – But what are we going to do about legal representation? / I'm worried etc etc

SQ 25 - AUDIO CUE – AUJARD ENTRANCE / THUNDERBOLT / DRUMS.

CHRIS AUJARD ENTERS - *dressed in an outrageous suit and shades, he has a permanent arsehole grin on his face (if he can be unclipping a parachute from his suit, even better).*

**AUJARD** – Chris Aujard here, I'll be taking over as legal council for the Post Office. (*big swoon & sigh from all ladies*) And may I just say ladies, that Horizon is VERY ROBUST!

**VENNELLS** – So good of you to parachute in. Mr Aujard, you've got the job.

**AUJARD** – I'm happy to be here, especially as my hourly rate was approved. So I understand you might be in a bit of a pickle with Horizon over some of your convictions?

**VENNELLS** – Yes, and as a deeply religious women of incredible conviction, I feel I must embrace the true teachings of the bible...

**AUJARD** – Exactly, be neither humble, nor forgiving - that's the right spirt!

**CROWE** – Look, this whole thing is nothing but a bunch of thieving failed coppers and retired publicans who were all on the take.

**LYONS** – But for reasons we cannot fathom in their interim report, Second Sight appear to be siding with these criminals. I mean they were hired to exonerate us.

**AUJARD** – Don't worry. In this situation I want you all to remember the golden rule: Keep calm and call counsel. Repeat after me – Keep calm and call counsel.

**EVERYONE** – Keep calm and call counsel...

**AUJARD** – I see my role as being one of stall the enemy, mire them in legal quagmire up to their neck, oh and lots of invoicing. Clean and sweep so to speak.

**LYONS** – What about our mediation process with the Subpostmasters?

**AUJARD** – Fuck the mediation process! End it and bury them in legal fees. It will mean a huge amount of overtime on my part of course, but that is a cross I will just have to bear, I'm afraid.

**VENNELLS** – The emperor chooses his people wisely, you're most welcome here Mr Aujard. So everyone is clear on our purpose. Protect Horizon, protect the brand, discredit Second Sight and stall the mediation process.

**EVERYONE** – Yes / very clear! / This body is rather heavy... etc etc

**BOGERD** – If I could just bring something up, because I am so brilliant and hard working, didn't I mention that before?

**EVERYONE** – Yes, you did.

**BOGERD** – Well I am completely transparent. I've heard that Panorama are making a programme that will be critical of Horizon and they're already interviewing several Subpostmasters.

**EVERYONE** (Improvised) Oh shit really? / I hadn't heard that / Can the BBC do that? / I'm brilliant... etc etc

**VENNELLS** – Silence!

*EVERYONE abruptly stops talking.*

**VENNELLS** – There is no need to panic. This is why we have Mr Aujard. We will continue the Post Office party line - that there are no IT failures within Horizon that could cause any financial shortfalls, and that the system is working brilliantly.

**CROWE** – Sorry, I know we're jumping around in the time line a bit, but if we intend to keep this secret committee secret, can we please call it something more innocuous than project X?

**AUJARD** – Good idea. How about Project Mop and Bucket?

**VENNELLS** – Too specific. Something more banal.

**BOGERD** – I've been told I'm very banal... and brilliant.

**LYONS** – I know, let's name it after an animal. How about a bird? Project Robin Redbreast.

**PERKINS** – Project Eagle?

**VENNELLS** – God no, far too American. Something more insignificant...

**BOGERD** (Still straining with the body) Project Sparrow?

**VENNELLS** – Perfect. Project Sparrow.

**EVERYONE** – Project Sparrow! Yes very good etc.

**BOGERD** – See, I'm brilliant and completely transparent.

*BOGERD EXITS*

**VENNELLS** – Now, I have granted the leaders of the Alliance an audience. Soon they will learn they have underestimated the resolve of the Empire, (afterthought) of the Post Office.

*SNAP TO BLACK – EVERYONE EXITS.*

*POSTMASTERS 4B (or 1) & 5 RE ENTER, crossing stage, stopping briefly.*

**POSTMASTER 4B** – So how was the meeting with the new CEO of the Post Office?

**POSTMASTER 5** – You were right. She's a cunt.

**POSTMASTER 4B** – So what now?

**POSTMASTER 5** – We take the cunts to court.

**POSTMASTER 4B** – About bloody time!

*SQ 26 - MUSIC / AUDIO CUE – SHARP SCENE CHANGE SOUND.*

**18) A BUNCH OF MUPPETS**

*IAN HENDERSON ENTERS.*

**HENDERSON** - One of the first things I learned when visiting darkest Bracknell, was there was quite a large team of Post Office staff working on the Horizon system, that were based at Fujitsu. It was quickly evident most of them were a right bunch of muppets.

*FUJITSU MUPPETS 1 & 2 ENTER/APPEAR (Post Office staff at Fujitsu) looking dazed and confused. (For how these speak, see 'The Aliens' from the Sesame Street TV series).*

**HENDERSON** – And having spoken to them, it was quickly apparent that no one within the senior management knew whose responsibility they were or what they were doing.

**FUJITSU MUPPET 1** – I don't know who we report to? Do you?

**FUJITSU MUPPET 2** – Nope, nope, nope.

**FUJITSU MUPPET 1/2** – (Joining in) Nope, nope, nope

**FUJITSU MUPPET 2** - Let's just keep writing code and take the money.

**FUJITSU MUPPETS** (both) – Yup yup, yup, yup, yup!!!!!!

*The MUPPETS appear to follow HENDERSON with their eyes as he moves.*

**HENDERSON** – After a brief tour of the place, I had an hour-long meeting with Gareth Jenkins, who had been an expert witness in one of the highest-profile court cases against a former Subpostmaster. You might say that what he'd said in court on behalf of the Post Office, and what he told me, were somewhat at odds with each other.

*GARETH JENKINS ENTERS, white, male age 40-60.*

**HENDERSON** – So just to be clear there is no remote access via Horizon to individual branch accounts by you or anyone in your team?

**JENKINS** – You're joking right? Hahahahahahaha....

**FUJITSU MUPPETS** (both) – Hahahahahahahahahah – He is funny. Hahahahahahaha.

**HENDERSON** – Right, so absolutely no access then?

**FUJITSU MUPPETS** (both) – No... nope, nope, nope, nope....

**JENKINS** – Of course we've got remote access, we couldn't do our job without it!

**FUJITSU MUPPETS** (both) – Yeah, that's right. Yup, yup, yup, yup.

**HENDERSON** – Explain to me how it works in layman's terms.

**JENKINS** – Basically we can log in as a Subpostmaster, take control of their terminals, and download a clone of their machine to work on.

**HENDERSON** – And you can basically do this with any branch at any time, anywhere in the country?

**JENKINS** – Absolutely!

**FUJITSU MUPPETS** (both) – Yeah, that's right. Yup, yup, yup, yup.

**HENDERSON** – And the Post Office knows this?

**FUJITSU MUPPETS** (both) – No, nope, nope, nope, nope...

**JENKINS** – Of course they do...

**FUJITSU MUPPETS** (both) – Yup! Yup! Yup! Yup! Yup!

**JENKINS** – We're not supposed to mention it to anyone outside the office....

**FUJITSU MUPPETS** (both) – No, no, no, no, no....

**JENKINS** – But you know that, right?

*JENKINS & MUPPETS EXIT.*

**HENDERSON** – Right... so there it was – from the mouths of their own design team, but it wasn't just the fault of Fujitsu. It was the conduct of the Post Office security and auditing teams. Our investigations discovered their entire approach focused on charging the defendant with a crime, rather than investigating if there had actually been one in the first place. Once a conviction was achieved it was entirely about asset recovery. Worse, they were incentivised to adopt this.

*ALWEN LYONS ENTERS (Holding a MUPPET, which she hides).*

**HENDERSON** – Back at POL HQ, I happened to bump into Post Office Secretary Alwen Lyons, telling her of my findings regarding remote access.

**LYONS** – You must have misunderstood, Ian.

**HENDERSON** – No misunderstanding, they gave me a demonstration.

**LYONS** – That's impossible Ian. There is no question of remote access. It simply can't happen.

**HENDERSON** – I saw it with my own eyes, and that's Mr Henderson to you. Gareth Jenkins demonstrated it to me himself.

**LYONS** – I'm sure he just meant it was theoretically possible to do it, not actually possible. I have to go, I have a secret meeting... I mean a normal meeting, to attend.

*LYONS exits.*

**HENDERSON** – There it was – wilful denial of the facts. After my conversation with Lyons, the Post Office made everything more difficult for me and Ron. We weren't passed on vital emails, or important documents. It was almost as if they had no interest in getting to the truth. When they got wind that our interim reports weren't going in their favour, they did everything they could to hinder our investigation. Documents we needed to see were kept from us under the guise of legal privilege, which contradicted the letter they'd sent out. The Post Office hierarchy appeared to forget they were public servants and were living in a blissful state of cultural blindness, but it was obvious they were going to try and discredit our report. When we published it they rejected all of our findings, and so Second Sight and Post Office Limited parted ways.

*HENDERSON EXITS / POSTMASTER 4 ENTERS.*

*SQ 27 - MUSIC CUE – ATMOS MOOD TRACK (MONOLOGUES).*

### *19) CASUALTIES OF WAR*

**POSTMASTER 4** - While others were fighting the good the fight, I was charged with three counts of False Accounting. My lawyer, she was a nice young lady, but I don't think she was that experienced. She advised me to plead guilty to the False Accounting charge and pay back the money. Where was I going to get £50,000? The Post Office asked the judge for a confiscation order so they could take my property but the Judge was wary, he requested actual paperwork verifying the amounts that were missing, but they failed to provide him with anything. I finally received a suspended prison sentence, and had to carry out 200 hours of unpaid work. But I still owed £50,000, so I had to get a second mortgage. I tried to not let my children see me cry, and we stopped having people over for barbecues. It was so hard after that, I just couldn't face seeing anyone. I didn't even take my children to school any more, because I was so ashamed. I might not have gone to prison but the Post Office turned my life into one all the same.

*POSTMASTER 4 EXITS / FUJITSU IT ENTERS.*

**FUJITSU IT** – Wow. It's all getting a bit heavy bruv, you know what I mean? I bet you're all relieved to see me again, in-it? Here, so this will interest you. With Horizon now running, or, you know, not running so well, if you get me, for over a decade, at one point there was a series of unplanned complete system shutdowns, which led to the entire Horizon network going off line for a whole day! I shit you not! At one point there was a million accounting issues in a single week bruv! A million. Not long after that an internal IT review was conducted. To put it into perspective, between its launch in 1999 and 2019 Fujitsu changed the operating software for Horizon 19,842 times. I know, right? I only need to download Bit Torrent once to fuck up my computer. Anyway, some time later we all got this email stating quite clearly that some of the recent issues with Horizon might have resulted in miscarriages of justice in ongoing court cases for the Post Office. Until I saw that memo I really had no idea what had been going on. We were all a bit disconnected from these things, but I think that's the way Fujitsu liked it. That memo soon disappeared from the work email account, but I'd already forwarded it to myself. I've always found its good to keep an eye on one's back in this line of work, you know what I mean. I ain't being no one's scapegoat, especially when I've been pointing out all the issues to them from day one. Them choosing to ignore my advice, that ain't on me bruv. When I realised people were suffering, really suffering, I knew it was time to blow the whistle innit.

*FUJITSU IT EXITS / MUSIC ENDS HERE (Manual Fade).*

*POSTMASTERS 1, 2 ENTER – they sit. POSTMASTER 5 ENTERS last, reading over some notes.*

**POSTMASTER 1** – I knew the mediation scheme was going to be a complete waste of time! They're just constantly stalling us.

**POSTMASTER 2** – I could tell they were never serious. They're probably hoping half of us will be dead before we see any compensation.

**POSTMASTER 1** - At least our good friend James Arburthnot MP expressed his disappointment with the attitude of the Post Office in the House of Commons.

**POSTMASTER 2** – Yes and it was even nicer finally seeing that Paula Vennells squirm in front of that BIS committee last week.

**POSTMASTER 1** – God I hope she ends up in the dock. Is Julian coming along today?

**POSTMASTER 2** – I heard he's hasn't been well again. We should send him a hamper from Harrods or something.

*POSTMASTER 4B ENTERS – (Dressed differently from their speech as PM4).*

**POSTMASTER 4B** – I'm not sure he's got much of an appetite. It's the chemo. Still, at least all the publicity has further swelled our ranks. Just goes to show some people do still watch Panorama. I heard the Post Office were very disappointed with the programme.

**POSTMASTER 2** – I certainly hope so. How's our correspondence on the website?

**POSTMASTER 1** – I can't keep up with all the emails, its hard to believe we've over 500 members now. We'll have to hold our next AGM in a bigger hall.

**POSTMASTER 2** – Makes you wonder how many more of us are out there. You're very quiet today Mr Smith.

**POSTMASTER 5** – I've got some good news. (pause) I've been using the time we've spent on the mediation process to assemble all the documentation we need for our case.

**POSTMASTER 1** – Our case?

**POSTMASTER 5** – We're going to sue the Post Office in the High Court.

**POSTMASTER 2** – Isn't that going to be expensive?

**POSTMASTER 5** – It is, but we've found a finance company who is willing to back us.

**POSTMASTER 4B** – Yes! (goes full Alan Partridge) Back of the net!

**POSTMASTER 1** – Who are they?

**POSTMASTER 5** – Therium, and they will back our case to the hilt, but the downside is they will take a huge portion of the money if we win.

**POSTMASTER 2** – When we win Mr Smith.

**POSTMASTER 5** – That's right. When we win. The way I see it, this is the only choice going forwards.

**EVERYONE** – Agreed.

**POSTMASTER 5** - Now we need to get as many of the members to sign up for this Group Litigation as possible.

**POSTMASTER 4B** – I'll get emailing everyone tonight Mr Smith.

**POSTMASTER 5** – Excellent Ms Smith. But remember, if we do this, everyone has to accept the outcome, whatever it maybe. Everyone has to go into this knowing they might not get everything they feel they deserve, and no doubt our good friends at the Post Office will deliberately make this drawn out and complicated.

*POSTMASTER 2 takes a phone call.*

**POSTMASTER 4B** – What's new? I'm game.

**POSTMASTER 1** – We've already been campaigning for six years, I'm in this for as long as it takes.

**POSTMASTER 2** (Into the phone) Yes... I understand. Of course, just let us know.

*POSTMASTER 2 looks in shock as they hang up the call.*

**POSTMASTER 5** – What is it?

**POSTMASTER 2** – It's Julian... he's gone...

*SQ 28 - MUSIC CUE – MONOLOGUES ATMOS TRACK.*

*POSTMASTER 5 stands.*

*POSTMASTERS 1, 2, 4B EXIT SLOWLY.*

**POSTMASTER 5** – So in August 2016, with 198 claimants on board, Bates v Post Office, that should probably be Smith v Post Office for tonight's purposes, was finally filed. It was the beginning of an extremely long road and ultimately there would be 555 of us. One of the unexpected upsides of this whole experience was I got to make friends with all these people I never would have met otherwise. My right hand man, Julian Wilson was one of them. We haven't had the time to introduce you to him tonight and if he was portrayed, he'd be dashingly handsome, much like that chap in the third row. If I was the head of our Alliance, Julian was very much it's beating heart. He'd been accepted onto the mediation scheme, only to be told as he was a convicted criminal, so the Post Office wouldn't mediate with him. As with many of us, the stress of it all impacted his health. First diabetes, and then, cancer. He told me he was going to beat it, and still came to as many meetings as he could. His smile was infectious. When he couldn't attend, he'd be on the phone to me. 'Do you need me to write any letters this week?' He'd say. With Julian it was always about what he could do for other people. We lost him the same month we filed our case in court. (beat) I... I can't believe he won't be around to see this through with the rest of us. I have to admit I feel like I've... lost my right arm. As the leader of our cause I've always had to put up a front, not being a man prone to showing emotion in public you understand. This fight for the truth, it took its toll and his loss was felt by us all. I just couldn't afford to show I was hurting, such are the burdens of leadership. So I would bottle it all up, and let these things out when I was alone. After his passing, now, more than ever I was determined to see us through to victory, no matter how long it took. But even I couldn't have predicted just how far the Post Office would go to try and derail our case.

*MUSIC FADES HERE / POSTMASTER 5 EXITS.*

**22) DERAILING TACTICS**

*LYONS, PERKINS, CROWE, AUJARD, BOGERD ENTER – they sit.*

**PERKINS** – I can't believe the gall of those Subpostmasters! Taking our country's most trusted brand to court. The bloody cheek of it. Who do they think they are?

**CROWE** – I think it's become a bit of cottage industry with everyone trying their luck.

**BOGERD** – Well I think I did brilliantly in front of the Committee.

**LYONS** – That's because you hardly said anything and when you did people couldn't hear you.

**BOGERD** – Exactly. I was very quiet and completely transparent.

*VENNELLS ENTERS – Everyone stands, then sits.*

**VENNELLS** – I certainly hope I do not have to take the stand. So what is our legal strategy for the court case Mr Aujard?

**AUJARD** – Lady Vennells, our legal team will object and delay at every stage. That is the plan, delay, delay, delay. Even though they have financial backing, I doubt their pockets are as deep as the Post Office. I mean, if my invoices don't make a dent, POL should be able to handle anything. Now remember what I said ladies – Keep calm and...

**EVERYONE** – Call counsel.

**CROWE** – But this is still going to cost us and it's not going to help our goal of becoming profitable by 2020.

**VENNELLS** – Nothing must derailed project 2020!

**EVERYONE** – No /Quite right / Yes 2020 is very important / I'm brilliant etc etc

**AUJARD** – However, I think I should warn you that as much as the Panorama programme lacked anything of real substance, we are going to have to admit that remote access to Horizon accounts in branches is possible.

**EVERYONE** – Oh no it isn't!

**AUJARD** – Well I'm afraid the defence have documents that definitely prove it is possible, so we would be wise to admit that and move on. Our team will ensure that you were all technically unaware of this of course.

**VENNELLS** – Fine. Do we have any other tricks up our sleeve?

**AUJARD** – Oh absolutely. Wherever possible we shall lay the blame at the door of Fujitsu.

**EVERYONE** – Yes all the fault of Fujitsu / Pearl Harbour / Never told us etc etc

**VENNELLS** – Excellent. You have done well Mr Aujard.

**AUJARD** – I aim to please and invoice.

**PERKINS** – Right shall we reconvene after the initial legal skirmishes have taken place?

**EVERYONE** – Sounds good / Excellent / I'm brilliant etc etc.

*SNAP TO BLACK – 2 seconds / LIGHTS BACK UP – Committee are still in situ.*

**PERKINS** – So now the initial legal skirmishes have taken place, where are we?

**AUJARD** – In the shit! I'm afraid some of you will have to take the stand, including you Angela.

**BOGERD** – Oh bollocks.

**PERKINS** – Oh, is that the time?

*SNAP TO BLACK 2 seconds / cast are still in situ. (except PERKINS who has exited)*

**LYONS** – I'm getting the impression in the court that the judge has taken a dislike to us...

**BOGERD** – I thought I defended Horizon rather brilliantly!

**AUJARD** – (Insincere) Yes... I don't think you won us any favours with the judge when you said that Horizon Error Logs, which I might add you had previously stated did not exist, were not relevant to the case.

**CROWE** – So what's the plan now?

**AUJARD** – They've a long way to go yet, and I have a brilliant plan to try and recuse the judge from the case.

**LYONS** – Really? For what reason?

**AUJARD** - For showing an obvious bias towards the defence.

**LYONS** – Do you think that will work?

**AUJARD** – Oh absolutely.

*SNAP TO BLACK 2 seconds / LIGHTS BACK UP – cast are still in situ.*

**CROWE** – So did it work?

**AUJARD** – No.

**BOGERD** – Bollocks. That's not very brilliant is it?

**LYONS** – So what happens now?

**AUJARD** – We succeeded in delaying the trial further. I doubt we'll be back in court again in 2019. Just one more matter, erm, I am reluctant to say this Ms Vennells, but the boss requires a meeting with you, in their office. Now.

**VENNELLS** – I see. Right, I shall see you all at the Bedfordshire bake sale then.

*VENNELLS EXITS.*

**AUJARD** – As we push on into 2020, I have a feeling this 'Corona Virus' issue might have the fortunate impact of delaying their case even further, thus keeping us off the front page. In the meantime I will just continue to invoice and you should all just keep calm...

**EVERYONE** – And call counsel!

*NARRATOR (& JUDGE) ENTER – SPARROW COMMITTEE (minus Perkins) move to stage left, staying in situ.*

*If not a voiceover, the JUDGE stands in the middle, with POL on one side, and the ALLIANCE on the other.*

### 23) JUDGEMENT DAY

*SQ 29 - MUSIC CUE – MONOLOGUE ATMOS TRACK 2.*

**NARRATOR** – Despite the best efforts of the Post Office to derail proceedings, eventually the case was heard, and in November 2019 the Post Office lost their appeal against the judgement. The judges sitting on the case did not mince their words.

*POSTMASTERS 1, 2, 4 & 5 ENTER – standing, wearing covid masks, listening to the judge. (This may be an audio recording).*

**JUDGE** – Today is the final hearing day of the Post Office litigation case, and I find as follows. Firstly, I have very grave concerns about the veracity of evidence given by Fujitsu employees both before me, and to other courts in previous proceedings. They consistently failed to disclose the existence of bugs and defects within the Horizon system, despite being fully aware of them. Consequently, I shall be referring this matter to the Director of Public Prosecutions for further investigation. Furthermore, I find the first iteration of the Horizon system was not remotely robust and its second incarnation, Legacy Horizon which came into operation in 2010, was slightly more robust but still had significant bugs, errors and defects. Furthermore, both the Post Office and Fujitsu failed to properly and fully investigate the myriad of ongoing problems with the Horizon system. All evidence in this trial, shows not only was there potential for such errors to occur but that it actually happened on numerous occasions. The approach of Post Office Limited to the litigation amounted to bare assertions and denials that ignore what has actually occurred. This amounts to the twenty-first century equivalent of maintaining the world is flat.

*Embarrassed, SPARROW members EXIT during the latter half of the speech. The POSTMASTERS share a hug and congratulations.*

HENDERSON & NARRATOR ENTER / POSTMASTERS EXIT.

**HENDERSON** – When Ron and I heard about the judgement, it immediately occurred to us both that if the Subpostmasters hadn't stolen anything, where had all the money recovered by the Post Office gone to? When is the Post Office going to return these funds back to their rightful owners? We couldn't help but think if the Post Office had simply acted on our report in 2015, it would have saved huge amounts of public money and spared a great many people considerable distress, loss and suffering. I was pleased to hear the 555 Subpostmasters were awarded 55 million pounds in compensation, but after legal fees I was sure glad I didn't have the job of working out who got what from the meagre pile that remained.

MUSIC FADES OUT.

**NARRATOR** – Legal proceedings continued into 2020, with the Post Office setting up the historical shortfall scheme, known to many currently as 'the long wait scheme', to compensate the former Subpostmasters. Several died while awaiting their compensation and most have yet to receive anything. More and more convictions were quashed and when POL decided it would no longer contest the remaining 44 of the cases in the Court of Appeal, they clearly saw which way the wind was blowing. But attitudes within the hierarchy still remained largely unchanged. Angela Van Den Bogerd told the High Court she still couldn't see any connection between the 500 Subpostmaster cases that even her own employer now said were unsafe. After leaving POL, Bogerd would go on being considerably less than brilliant in a number of other roles. Finally the government ordered a public inquiry. It's still going on / it's just finished (change as appropriate). In the mean time Paula Vennells stepped down as CEO of Post Office Ltd and became something of a persona non grata in her other roles. We can only hope that one day she will be sitting in the dock herself. You know, I often wondered how she would fare if she had to face a lie detector test. Shall we find out?

*NARRATOR EXITS.*

**24) TRUTH OR LIE...**

*SQ 30 MUSIC CUE – GAME SHOW JINGLE INTO HEARTBEAT ATMOS (The music has a vibe similar to Who Wants to be a Millionaire).*

*VENNELLS & MAX PENALTY ENTER wheeling small podiums/lecterns onto stage.*

*PENALTY is best described as the love child of Ted Rogers, Derek Acora & Bob Monkhouse. He wears a loud jacket and has a spinning bow tie.*

**PENALTY** – Welcome ladies and gentleman to another game of Truth or Lie, with me your host Max Penalty, and tonight our lovely guest, Executive Chairman, Paula Vennells... CBE, I know what the 'C' in that stands for. Here we go Ms Vennells, your starter for ten.

**VENNELLS** – Where am I? Is this some kind of dream?

**PENALTY** – For legal reasons we're going to say yes. Now, were you aware of an internal Post Office report that stated, in regard to the conviction of Subpostmaster Jo Hamilton, that there was no evidence of actual theft?

**VENNELLS** – No, I was not aware of that report.

*SQ 31 AUDIO CUE – BUZZER.*

**PENALTY** – I'm afraid that's a lie. As CEO, it was part of your duty to have been made aware of such reports. Having taken over as CEO, everyone told you that Horizon was reliable but were you not informed that Horizon had systemic issues from an important source?

**VENNELLS** – No, everyone I relied on told me Horizon was without fault.

*SQ 31 AUDIO CUE – BUZZER.*

**PENALTY** – I'm afraid that's a lie. Tim McCormack detailed this issue to you in a 2015 email...

**VENNELLS** – Well... I... he was just a Subpostmaster.

**PENALTY** – Of course, they only run the entire network of the business, we understand you weren't interested in what they had to say. Let's move on shall we. Again, not long after your promotion to CEO, a company called BAE systems furnished the Post Office with what became known as 'The Deltica Report'. That report stated among other things, that Horizon had 'insecure systems and processes', 'inconsistent audits' , and a 'lack of robust controls and records.' Did you feel secure pressing forwards with the criminal convictions of your Subpostmasters after having been informed of this?

**VENNELLS** – I never saw the content of that report when I took over as CEO.

*SQ 31 AUDIO CUE – BUZZER.*

**PENALTY** – That is another lie. It was discussed at a board meeting over which you presided. We've seen the redacted minutes...

**VENNELLS** – But as I said I never saw it.

*SQ 31 AUDIO CUE – BUZZER.*

**PENALTY** – I'm sorry Ms Vennells, but our bullshit detector disagrees with you. An expert report questioning Horizon's reliability, was deliberately hidden from the counsel for the defence in more than one of your court cases. Truth or lie?

**VENNELLS** – Lie - We wouldn't have deliberately held back any evidence.

*SQ 31 AUDIO CUE – BUZZER.*

**PENALTY** – I'm afraid that is true, the Post Office constantly withheld anything from the defence in your court cases, which would show that Horizon could be at fault. You're doing very well Ms Vennells. Moving on, more recently you had to step away from a number of high profile positions, including the boards of the NHS Trust, Morrisons, Dunelm, the Post Office of course, and your position within the Church of England. Was it your decision to do so?

**VENNELLS** – Absolutely, the proceedings of the court case had become a distraction for me to properly fulfil my duties in those roles.

*SQ 31 AUDIO CUE – BUZZER.*

**PENALTY** – That is a lie, I believe in every case you were told your position was no longer tenable, and you should leave quietly.

**VENNELLS** – That's absolutely not true. The decision was reached in mutual agreement.

**PENALTY** – We shall let the court of public opinion decide on that one. After the complete vindication of the first 39 Subpostmasters, you have said you offered the innocent Subpostmasters a full apology. True or a lie?

**VENNELLS** – Yes that is true, I remember exactly what I said - 'I was deeply saddened by the Subpostmasters accounts heard during the Court of Appeals proceedings, and I am truly sorry for the suffering caused to them as a result of convictions, which the Court of Appeal has today overturned.

*SQ 31 AUDIO CUE – BUZZER.*

**PENALTY** – I'm sorry Ms Vennells, I'm afraid that might be your words, but I have been informed that no Subpostmaster considers that a full nor sincere apology. During your time in the pulpit, you said and I quote: Give to your servant an understanding heart that I may discern between good and evil...'

**VENNELLS** – Yes that's right.

**PENALTY** – Do you think you have an understanding heart Ms Vennells?

**VENNELLS** – Of course.

*SQ 32 MUSIC CUE END KLAXON / HEARTBEAT THEME ENDS HERE.*

**PENALTY** – Look at that we're out of time, so I guess we'll never know! At the end of that round you've scored nil points Ms Vennells, but have yet to face justice. Fortunately you left the Post Office with a golden parachute on top of your yearly salary of £255,000. Didn't she do well ladies and gentleman?

**VENNELLS** – I think I've just had a terrible nightmare.

**PENALTY** – Trust me Ms Vennells, I think for you it's just beginning.

*VENNELLS & PENALTY EXIT / POSTMASTERS 1, 2, 4 & 5 ENTER.*

*SQ 33 - MUSIC CUE – MONOLOGUES ATMOS TRACK.*

## 25) VICTORY SPEECHES

**POSTMASTER 1** – It was an odd experience, us all fighting the good fight for so long and going back and forth to court during the Pandemic, knowing we couldn't even hug each other. After the first judgement was handed down, vindicating our cause, we couldn't really celebrate, because of social distancing. Although personally I think our party would have qualified as a work event. So we'd won, but the money didn't go very far. Most of the 555 barely got back a fraction of what they'd lost and thousands more have now joined the new mediation scheme. Part of the problem is that the perception of the general public is that we won and this whole thing is over.

Nothing could be further from the truth. We're still battling for the full amount of money that they stole from us to be returned. So even after everything we've been through, still it goes on. It's hard to describe how I felt after it all. Emotional, but not joyful. To get joy out of life once again, yeah, was going to take me some time.

*POSTMASTER 1 EXITS.*

**POSTMASTER 5** - The Post Office were finally forced to admit that at least 500 Subpostmasters may have been wrongly convicted using Horizon evidence and believe me, there will be many more to come. In December of 2020 the first six convictions were quashed, dozens more would follow including several this year alone. In the fallout that followed, a pattern of Fujitsu and the Post Office blaming each other for their mutual failures continues even now. The testimony of some of their employees at the public inquiry beggars belief. You can see it for yourselves on YouTube. Looking back, I never wanted the last third of my life to be consumed by running a campaign for Justice. I never wanted to lead 555 individuals in a legal battle for compensation, nor be party to how compensation might be divided up accordingly. That was and still is a source of some difficulty for many. I didn't want to watch my good friend... our friend, Julian, lose his battle to cancer. I'd give up every penny of my compensation, just to have him standing here with me now, and if it hadn't been for the actions of the Post Office, I am sure he would be. For some our legal victory has been hollow, and I know many are still upset and feel they were not paid enough. I cannot disagree with them. Still, I'm proud of everything we achieved, bringing the scandal to light and making a difference. We fought the good fight and now I think it's time for me to put my feet up.

**MRS BATES** (Offstage) – Alan! Your tea's ready. I've got The Professionals lined up.

**POSTMASTER 5** – Ah... My favourite episode I hope?

**MRS BATES** – Private Madness, Public Danger...

**POSTMASTER 5** – Quite. Coming Mrs Smith. Any chance of some biscuits?

*POSTMASTER 5 EXITS.*

**POSTMASTER 4** – My conviction was finally overturned in the summer of 2021. It took so long and after everything they had put me and my family through, I am still waiting for a full and proper apology. Not one that begins with the words 'it is a matter of regret..'. My oldest child was twelve when this all started. They're twenty-nine now and it's still going on because they keep stalling over compensation. Now we have this public inquiry, which is good, and I was glad I got to speak to Sir Wyn, but do they have any real power? Even if they recommend criminal prosecutions, I can't see the guilty parties going to prison. You know they'll just play the blame game and then drag it out in the courts as long as possible, just like they're doing now with our so-called compensation. You know what will happen then, everyone's lawyers will claim that too much time has passed and it's better for everyone to just move on. I've been trying to move on for two decades, so don't talk to me about moving on. Because believe me I'm trying, but they just won't let me, with all these games they keep playing with our lives. This is one of the worst acts of wanton criminal behaviour in the history of our country, and they think they're going to get away with it. Are you going to let them? My daughter has just become a lawyer, imagine that. She told me the other day 'Muma, I'm never going to let them forget what they did to you... you wait and see.' Like I said, wise beyond her years, my daughter.

*POSTMASTER 2 hugs POSTMASTER 4, who EXITS.*

**POSTMASTER 2** – With my conviction quashed, our celebration was somewhat muted. Because we followed the social distancing rules, because that's what lawful people do. Follow the rules. One thing I've realised throughout this awful journey is that people who come from certain walks of life, think that rules just don't apply to them. When I look in the mirror now, I cannot believe how much I have aged. This hair was a lovely shade of blonde once - now my youngest calls me

Gandalf. I was just twenty three when I went to prison. Looking at myself now, I feel like I'm sixty-three. That was the worst thing the Post Office took from me – time. You can't ever get that back. It's gone forever. It's hard to know where to place all the anger we have sometimes, because I am so angry. So we'd all met each other and shared our mutual horror stories, we finally had the true picture of the devastation this catastrophic mess has caused in people's lives. Hundreds of marriages, relationships and reputations ruined. My friend is right, it would be overly optimistic of us to think that those responsible for all that we endured would actually see the inside of a prison cell. But I was pleased to learn some of those responsible at the Post Office have deep religious convictions. That's good. I've always been a big believer in karma. If there's a Heaven, then their place truly belongs in hell.

**26) THE PEARLY GATES (This scene was deleted in 2023)**

*SQ 34 - MUSIC CUE – CHOIR OF ANGELS (previous track ends here).*

*The COMPANY ENTER, including both AUDITORS, now dressed in white, wearing shades, who stand by the pearly gates. One member of the company (TBC) holds up a sign which reads: Heaven sometime in The Future.*

*THE GATEKEEPER ENTERS, holding a clipboard and pen – (This character will be a famous individual, that suits the actor, known for a positive contribution to humanity, ie Nelson Mandela/Lady Diana or similar).*

*The COMPANY form a queue to get into 'Heaven' with several of the POSTMASTERS waiting to get in, further back in the queue VENNELLS impatiently waits in line.*

**THE GATEKEEPER** – Right, who do we have on our heroes guest list today then?

**AUDITOR 2** – It's quite a long list my lady, there appears to be an awful lot of people coming in under the name Smith today.

**THE GATEKEEPER** – Let me see that. Ah yes, Tracy Falstead, Alan Bates, Seema Misra, Nicola Arch, Teju Adedayo, Rebecca Thompson from Computer Weekly, very good. Ah, Nick Wallis, he certainly knows how to write a good book, Mark Baker, there's even a couple of lawyers coming in. Gosh, it's very busy isn't it? This is a very long list, I don't have time to read them all out. Do we have enough Haloes for all these people?

**AUDITOR 1** – Yes my worship, as per our penance agreement we've been toiling away to complete them overnight sir.

**THE GATEKEEPER** – Quite right. Be a terrible shame if you'd have to spend all eternity being electrocuted in that accident you had in your pool in Marbella, wouldn't it? Right we'd best get on then. Next...

*An impatient disguised VENNELLS attempts to jump the queue.*

**VENNELLS** – I'm sure that I am supposed to be next.

**AUDITOR 1** – Oi! No pushing in! Get back in line.

**VENNELLS** – But I'm a former Anglican Priest! Surely I don't have to wait in line with these... these people.

**AUDITOR 1** – I don't care if you're Lady Diana. You'll wait in line like everyone else!

**AUDITOR 2** - Former priests always go straight to the back anyway.

*VENNELLS reluctantly retreats. POSTMASTER 5 steps forward.*

**THE GATEKEEPER** – Name?

**POSTMASTER 5** – (uncertainly) I think I might be under Mr Smith?

**THE GATEKEEPER** – Ah yes Alan Brrrr..... Smith. Well look at that, we haven't had anyone with this many gold stars next to their name in quite some time have we?

**AUDITOR 1** – We haven't, no my Lady.

**POSTMASTER 5** – Oh is that a good thing?

**THE GATEKEEPER** – Oh yes Mr Smith, and several others Smiths I see. You're booked first class from here on out. And how was your passing?

**POSTMASTER 5** – Oh very comfortable thank you. I was asleep and then I was here.

**THE GATEKEEPER** – We like to do what we can. Enter and know a life of peace. If you would show them to the Wilson-Griffith luxury accommodations.

**AUDITOR 1** – Very good my Lady. If your group would follow me please.

*AUDITOR 1 shows POSTMASTER 5 and all POSTMASTERS out, they EXIT. VENNELLS pushes to the front.*

**THE GATEKEEPER** – Name?

*VENNELLS attempts a different voice.*

**VENNELLS** – Mrs Smith...

*SQ34– ALARM - An alarm immediately sounds.*

*The AUDITORS rapidly RE-ENTER.*

**THE GATEKEEPER** – Look where you are Ms Vennells, you can't take the train to fibberton and get away with it around here I'm afraid.

**VENNELLS** – I meant I am a friend of Mrs Smith. I'm probably with the earlier party...

**THE GATEKEEPER** – Paula Vennells is it? Ah yes. Died in a bizarre gardening accident.

**VENNELLS** – Paula Vennells, CBE, that's right...

**THE GATEKEEPER** – Ah Yes. We've a special place reserved for you.

**VENNELLS** – Is it a penthouse? Or a recreation of my lovely Bedfordshire home?

**THE GATEKEEPER** – Not exactly. You'll spend your eternity with the Lord of the Underworld. Take her down to Sir Jimmy Saville...

**VENNELLS** – What? Noooooo!

**SAVILE (V.O)** – Now then, now then, now then, goodness gracious me, what have we here?

*AUDITOR 2 & VENNELLS EXIT / NARRATOR ENTERS.*

### 27) FINAL REVELATION

**NARRATOR** – Do not mistake the intent of the dark humour of our story tonight, to trivialise the pain and loss that hundreds upon hundreds experienced in this woeful tale. And do you know what contract Fujitsu have been awarded now? To give IT support to the National computer system for the Police Forces of the United Kingdom. An insider already tells us it's not working too well. I know, I'm speechless too. The Horizon Post Office Scandal became the biggest miscarriage of justice in British history. Destroying thousands of lives by the total indifference shown by people like Angela Van Den Bogerd, Alwen Lyons, Alice Perkins, Adam Crozier, Mark Davies and Paula Vennellls, CBE. Oh yes, they gave her that honor in 2019, even after the facts of this case were known. Because that's what we do now, reward people who lie and send innocent people to prison. You remember our man from Boeing at the beginning of our story? How just one person's voice could have saved lives? They had that chance to, but they didn't take it. No, they continued to sanction prosecutions, even after knowing Horizon was unsafe, knowing their actions were unlawful. You know, if you look up the word 'murder' in the dictionary, its literal meaning is this: *Intentional, unlawful, killing.* Thirty five Subpostmasters died before they could see justice. Four committed suicide. One of those was my father.

*SQ 35 - MUSIC CUE – FINAL NARRATOR TRACK.*

POSTMASTER 3 ENTERS, *still wearing his cricket pads, carrying his bat. He stands downstage from the NARRATOR, his stance proud. He looks at the NARRATOR, smiling as they speak.*

**NARRATOR** – Dad was a proud man. The Post Office could have taken everything else from him, and he could have handled it. He'd still be here today. Just not his pride.

*NARRATOR walks over to POSTMASTER 3, they turn and face one another, a look of great affection is exchanged between them.*

**NARRATOR** - When you took that, to use the definition of unlawful killing as far as I am concerned - you murdered him. Now he's gone. All the public inquiries, all their convoluted compensation schemes, won't bring him back. But if you're going to put a price on his life when you come to compensate my family, then you'd better be expecting to pay us millions. Not that it's about the money, but we know that's the only language you'll understand. It was more cost effective to prosecute the innocent than it was to fix some broken software and admit that you were wrong.

*ALL OTHER POSTMASTERS ENTER, line up upstage, behind the NARRATOR.*

**NARRATOR** – You see when the Post Office went after my father, it wasn't just about destroying his life and his family... my family. They looked at him and all the Subpostmasters they prosecuted as financial assets to be stripped. They were just goods to be evaluated and mined for every penny they had, until all that they owned, all that they once were, all that they had worked so hard to become, was taken from them. Until there was nothing left.

*ALL POSTMASTERS turn their backs to the audience.*

**NARRATOR** – To Post Office Ltd they were all the same. To us they were real people, look around, they could have been the person next to you, or your neighbour, they were fathers, mothers, brothers, sisters, friends, loved ones. We will remember them as the people they were before. The Post Office didn't count on us fighting back... so all of you who knew and were involved in this shameful atrocity, we're going to make sure people never forget what you did to us. That is our gift to you. It's your legacy after all. Consider it a promise, one that I made to my father. You don't know me yet, but you will. Believe me when I say, unlike the Post Office, our most trusted brand - I don't break my promises.

*SNAP TO BLACK.*

*CAST BOWS.*

**END**

.

# ACKNOWLEDGMENTS

Thanking everyone who enabled our show False Accounts to become a reality in 2022 is no short list but I shall do my best.

Firstly The Outcasts Creative production team for the original 2022 show: Dickon Tolson, Chris de Wilde, Suzette 'Pluckasaurus' Pluck, Ice 'Dib Dob' Dob, Roni Elson, Melissa 'Puppet Master' Stanton, Billy & Claire George and the staff of both The Old Joint Stock and Questors Theatres

My family - brother, Jason Flemyng, sisters, Sharon Sorrentino & Zoey Dixon. I love all three of you so, so much. Asha, Zuri (little miss big cheeks) and my in-laws, Alyson, Resty & Inni (Uncle Lance misses you so much)

The artistic creative teams of the OSO Arts Centre - Barnes, The Gatehouse Theatre - Highgate & The North Star Pub Finchley. Victoria 'Jeffers' Jeffrey.

The Critical Drinker (Will Jordan) & the Mods, Positive Fandom, La Reina Creole, Copa Cantania and the entire online community that have supported my efforts with The Outcasts Creative YouTube channel. Matthew Holmes & Gary Boulter of Outcasts Australia.

The entire cast & production teams of both the London and Birmingham shows & all those members of The Outcasts Creative who came to support the show. (names in the front of this book)

The other fighters of the cause - Computer Weekly, Karl Flinders, Mark Baker, Rebecca Thomson, Nick Wallace, Lord Arbuthnot, Ian Henderson, Ron Warmington, El Shaikh and no doubt many others.

*My sincere thanks to all those Postmasters who gave their support to the show, either verbally or by doing so in person, many of them travelling the length of the UK to do so. I will mention a few names with the caveat that no doubt I will almost certainly have missed someone. In no particular order - Wendy 'Buffers' Buffrey, Nicola 'Gobby' Arch, Siema Kamran & Kamran Ashraf, Tracy Felstead, Seema Misra, Janet Skinner, Tim Brentnall & partner, Lee Castleton, Tim McCormack, Huw Langridge, Kevin Brown, Gary Brown, Maria Lockwood, Della Ryan and I am sure many others.*

*My sincere apologies to anyone I've overlooked.*

*My parents, Barbra & Gunnar Nielsen - sadly they are not around to see this play, but I know they would have loved it.*

# ABOUT THE AUTHOR

Lance Steen Anthony Nielsen, (Leath Heaton, to use his African name) was brought up in Kingston-upon-Thames and Surbiton in Surrey. He was adopted, but raised by an English mother and Danish father. He enjoyed many a Danish themed Christmas in his childhood years. His Father, Gunnar Bang Nielsen, was a runner for the Danish resistance during World War 2, and was involved in hiding downed British airman, before smuggling them over to Sweden in fishing boats. His father travelled across the Sahara Desert after the war, hitching a ride on a convoy of trucks with the French Foreign Legion. Lance had a strong interest in this period of history from a young age, after hearing these stories and watching the films *The Longest Day* and *A Bridge Too Far*.

During his youth he spent much of his time playing historical miniature wargaming, rolling dice, renting videos, going to the cinema and forgetting to tell his mother what time he would be home when he went out. He studied Audio Visual Design at Epsom School of Art and Design (Now Surrey Institute of Art and Design) where his ambitious epic projects were often thwarted by his uninspiring tutors who would tell him to go and photograph 'Some hands' instead. He has still yet to do any photographic or film projects involving hands or indeed any other human appendage.

To support himself during and after college, he worked at his local cinema. His passion for watching movies would even result in him traveling to see more films in Central London on his day off, much to the incredulity of his fellow ushers, who thought this was just plain stupid. After a period of working in other retail jobs which barely warrant a mention of more than two lines, he started making films with any type of camera he could get his hands on and writing and directing plays for London's off West-End Theatre scene and also continued to act on stage and do occasional small roles in films.

He was the resident playwright for the Jacksons Lane Theatre from 1997 until 2002 where his first play 'Waiting for Hillsborough' won him the Best Talent in New Writing, at the Liverpool Arts and Entertainment Awards. Following on from this much of his work began to focus on topics set within social and political arenas. He would write and direct several original works over the next decade. His next play, 'Sticks and Stones', covered three families' lives over four decades during the conflict in Northern Ireland and brought him much critical acclaim. He also wrote it as a television series. 'The Victoria Climbie Inquiry' earned him *Time Out magazine Critics Choice*, while his play 'Making Time' won him a *Peter Brook Empty Space Award*.

  Additionally, he won a *Peggy Ramsay Award* and has had plays produced at The Hackney Empire, Bridewell, Landor, Lion and Unicorn, The Mask. The Stratford Arts and Old Red Lion Theatres. He also wrote & directed the play about the inquiry into The Marchioness Disaster. He recently just completed writing a play about the making of the original The Magnificent Seven movie entitled 'The Seven Young Guns of Hollywood'. He also directed both of the plays for Tom Hardy's short-lived Shotgun Theatre Company, 'Two Storm Wood' and 'Blue on Blue'. He was also an acting student at both Anna Scheers & Timber Theatre, the latter of which he also taught at. This led to him becoming an acting coach in later years, with a good knack for being able to read what was required by the Casting Director from audition scenes. He continues this role and coaches actors from all over the world.

In 2012 the advancement of digital technology enabled him to write and direct the indy low budget feature film 'The Journey' starring

Jason Flemyng and Lindsey Coulson which should not be confused with any of the other seven films on IMDB which share the same title. It has won numerous awards at various Film Festivals Worldwide, including bagging one for Lance as Best Director. Since then he has written numerous feature film & television screenplays including scripts about Colin Stagg, *Paratrooper* (About the first black Paratrooper in the British army) *Behind Closed Doors*, written for his friend Jason Flemyng and the pilot for *Diamonds In The Sky*, which he always conceived as a television series. After being unable to get in the room to pitch it to broadcasters, he decided to write it as a novel fiction/drama series to be told over six volumes, the first two books are available on Amazon.

More recently he wrote & co-directed the play *Borderlands* set in immigration at Heathrow, where the audience voted to release or detain the suspect in the narrative. His second stage production for The Outcasts Creative (7th in total) was *False Accounts*, telling the story of the *Horizon Post Office Scandal*, which he co-directed and wrote. He also acted in the show, and currently works as an acting coach, novelist, script editor and appraiser as well as doing Ghost Writing for biographies.

Lance has spent a considerable portion of his time in Greece, a country which he credits for 'Saving his life' during an impromptu visit during a very dark period of his life in the summer of 2009. The other person who has done the same on several occasions is his closest friend Jason Flemyng, who is the closet equivalent to an older brother he's ever had. He resides in North London alongside a rather large collection of Lego and numerous board games.

*'I've had more wins than losses in this crazy creative industry, but how much are you going to learn from someone who got the top with ease or got lucky on their first big break? The true passion in being a creative is in not giving up when the struggles are at their hardest. That takes real commitment and drive. You tell stories because you love it, you create characters*

*and journeys that people will find compelling. Above all you want an emotional response to your work. This is the greatest compliment of all to any story teller. Thank you for coming on this journey with me.'*

# ALSO BY LANCE STEEN ANTHONY NIELSEN

The Marchioness Inquiry

13 Seconds in Kent State

Sticks and Stones

Diamonds in the Sky Book 1 - Paraousia

Diamonds in the Sky Book 2 - The Orphans of Babylon

1988 - A journal of teenager and his visits to the cinema

Pegasus Bridge - The Screenplay

Paratrooper - The Screenplays - Episodes 7 & 8

Persecution - The Trail of Colin Stagg

Printed in Great Britain
by Amazon